# AMERICAN REFUGEE POLICY:
# ETHICAL AND RELIGIOUS REFLECTIONS

*Edited by*
*Joseph M. Kitagawa*

*Published by*
*The Presiding Bishops Fund*
*for World Relief,*
*The Episcopal Church*

*in collaboration with*
*Winston Press*

### *The Presiding Bishop's Fund for World Relief*
### *The Episcopal Church*

The Presiding Bishop's Fund for World Relief was founded
by the Episcopal Church in 1939 to help refugees fleeing
from pre-war Germany. Since that time the Fund's ministry
has grown to include programs of relief, rehabilitation, and
development, but refugee/migration concerns have always
remained a major focus. The Board of Directors of the Fund
is pleased to support the publishing of this volume and its
distribution in the Church in the earnest hope that persons of
all faiths will continue to honor a godly and moral heritage
through acts of grace and mercy to the "stranger in our
midst."

The Rev. Canon Samir J. Habiby, D.D.
Executive Director

Cover design: Terry Dugan

Library of Congress Catalog Card Number: 84-40507

ISBN: 0-86683-955-0 (paperback)
ISBN: 0-86683-975-5 (hardcover)

Printed in the United States of America

5   4   3   2   1

The publishing program of The Seabury Press is being continued by
Winston Press, Inc.
430 Oak Grove
Minneapolis, Minnesota 55403

# *Contents*

# Preface

## The Most Rev. John M. Allin, the Presiding Bishop of the Episcopal Church

The tragic phenomenon of refugees and displaced persons confronts with peculiar urgency and poignancy the consciences of all freedom-loving people, and especially religious men and women, throughout the world. To the Christian, the problem of forced migration symbolizes the intricate intertwining of human and religious issues.

Those of us who are North Americans, living on this continent committed to the principle of freedom and blessed with natural resources and ample space, often fail to appreciate the depth of the biblical exhortation: "Beloved, I beseech you as aliens and exiles . . ." (1 Peter 2:11).

The biblical message was written not only to the small band of persecuted forebears of our own faith community; it is addressed to all in our time, a reminder that we are not the ultimate masters of life. The faithful, however committed they may be, are bound to raise searching questions and to experience uncertainties in working out the implications of their faith. This is particularly true in the midst of the ambiguities of the social, economic, and political arenas of the national and global communities.

We heirs of the Anglican tradition remain committed to the worship, teaching, and witnessing tasks of the church. At the same time we recognize that these activities are but external manifestations of the fundamental vocation of the church to discern the will of God as faithful instruments of the *One* who became flesh in order to break down the barriers that separate this world from its Creator. It is God who calls us to confront honestly the phenomenon of refugees and others in need who are victims of political, economic, and social injustice and oppression.

The present volume is recommended to you not because it offers neat solutions but in the fervent hope that such a book will provoke you to more serious reflection on the global problem of refugees and uprooted people. Current patterns of forced migration affect the future of this world and our continent. We must be motivated, as our life is lived on this continent and in this nation, to explore not only a realistic and viable refugee and immigration policy but also a policy which reflects the ethical and humanitarian principles embedded in our life and history. As Archbishop William Temple reminds us, God's concern reaches beyond the realm of religion to all spheres of life. The refugees are, above all else, human; and, ". . . as you did it to one of the least of these my brethren. . . ." (St. Matthew 26:40).

The Presiding Bishop's Fund for World Relief, which serves as the general secretariat of the Religious Advisory Committee, has been in the forefront with ecumenical and interfaith colleagues in bringing before the church and public the international plight of refugees and displaced persons. Episcopal dioceses and hundreds of parishes have responded to the homeless through offers of sponsorship and support via the Fund. Reflections on migration and its root causes as related to U.S. national policy toward refugees and migrants should be contextually tied to this response of our church to the homeless and the stranger.

# *Foreword*

# Martin E. Marty

Libraries of small cities, small campuses, small churches, and great citizens include hundreds of books which include "ethical and religious reflections." This is likely to be the first such book about refugees on most of their shelves. Tattered, now, are the books which dealt with the ethics of labor organization from fifty years ago. The religious studies of racial themes and civil rights are abundant since they came to focus after mid-century. Reflections on war and peace after Vietnam and in the age of nuclear weapons find ready publishers, buyers, and readers.

Some of these books, though they deal with issues which seem insoluble and whose human costs are unimaginable, can press one solution or another on readers. A public does or does not assure certain rights to labor and management, to minorities who were once denied them. People are urged to "stay in" or "get out" of a Vietnam, to arm or disarm—though that last topic admits of frightfully important nuances and shadings.

By the middle of the 1980s, however, issues have presented themselves which do not present thoughtful citizens with simple this or that, yes or no, in or out decisions. Take the issue of population and hunger. No one contests the fact that the earth is capable of producing sufficient food for all. Yet controversies over development, dependency, and distribution touch on political and economic elements which complicate the issue until it seems insoluble. Even production of food is complex. Fail to use insecticides and see crops fail. Use insecticides and risk spreading cancer. In America, the religious public has grown sophisticated about these problems. One can get a discussion on triage in the quietest backwater town meetings and church or synagogue groups. There are evidences that the public has not lost all its heart. Ancient stories of the acts of God and enduring symbols of the sacred inspire people to want to act. How do they do so?

Few issues which will be with us through the end of this millennium dramatize the complexity more than the one which this pioneer symposium brings to focus: refugees. Author after author reminds us that being an exile, an alien, a displaced person is a primal anxiety for the settled, a constant religious image "ever since Adam," a perduring practical question, an issue which forces "ethical and religious reflection." Yet it seems to admit of no this or that, yes or no, answers.

The statistics are conveniently amassed in some of the testimony here. People speak of this as the century of displacement, the epoch of the refugee. Politics, war, famine, the many horsemen of our apocalypse, drive people from homes or never let them know any in the first place. Totalitarian wills care not at all for the aliens they create. Yet statistics alone are not compelling. Josef Stalin had good credentials for noting the second half of his famous saying: the death of a single person is a tragedy; the death of a million is a statistic.

So the authors move beyond mere reportage to the questions which nag responsive people in those town halls, churches, synagogues, or classrooms where moral and political issues draw reflection. They use the language of "limits," of "finitude," a language which reminds us that America cannot simply become the asylum for all people in need. The issue is how readily citizens will admit that and what they will do once they have recognized it.

As ethical and religious reflectors, however, the authors neither are contented with statistics and analyses nor ready to do no more than sit on the curbstone and weep. Something, some things, can be done. Those with biblical sweep and historical recall show how the godly and responsible have greeted and served the refugee through the ages. The philosophers and moralists make available some of the tools for addressing this issue, never forgetting that the reader who has given little previous thought to the subject will very quickly pose the right questions.

One element in favor of those who would do something about the refugee crisis in religious circles is this: something has been done. Despite their limited resources and vision, despite their temptation to apathy and their diffidence about politics or ineptness in dealing with international themes, Americans in synagogue and church have already drawn on the lore and impulses of their traditions. They have seen their hearts stirred, their hands moved to begin action. The religious vocabulary and program of today know something about "boat people" and other refugees. Believers can build on these timid beginnings.

Jacques Ellul once chided people of faith for showing interest only in "the fashionable poor." The fashionable poor draw media attention. Siding with them advances one's own political causes domestically. The refugee is unfashionable. Who profits from dealing with the Somalians, the Haitians? Yet, for all their drastic and valid differences, differences from which the reader benefits, the authors of this book will never let fashion determine the outcomes of ethical and religious thought and response. They state their case eloquently. It is time, high time, to hear them.

# An Invocation*

## Anthony J. Bevilacqua
## Bishop of Pittsburgh

Heavenly Father, it is through two of your most powerful lobbyists, Moses and Aaron, that the first immigration law for
refugees was enacted, when the Pharaoh let your persecuted but
chosen people leave the land of Egypt.

The first immigration law that you enacted for your chosen
people in their new land was not to mistreat the aliens living in
your land but to treat them as you would native sons and
daughters and love them as you would love yourselves.
"Remember, you were once aliens in the land of Egypt: I am the
Lord your God."

All of us are aliens on this earth, refugees seeking the eternal
safety, happiness, and peace of your heavenly land. Let us be
mindful that on this earthly pilgrimage we are all equal in your
sight. In your eye there are among us no kings, no queens, no
rich, no poor, no learned, no fools, no legal or illegal aliens, no
refugees, no natives.

On this journey, let us hold each other's hand, helping each
other each day to take another step towards you. For it is only
when we travel as brothers and sisters that we can reach your
home and there be forever your sons and daughters. Amen.

---

*The portions of this volume marked with asterisks are from the edited version
of the conference proceedings. For the rest, the contributors have revised their
statements for this volume.

# Introduction

Books on the subject of refugees are many and varied. Some concern the global aspect of the refugee problem; others concentrate on regional or national implications. Many depict social, economic, political, and legal ramifications; and not a few treat the human aspects of the tragic fate of refugees and practical considerations in alleviating their hardships. Although the purpose of this volume is more modest and the scope more limited than in these approaches, its intent is still basic and fundamental: it aims to probe into religiously inspired ethical and moral principles embedded in America's cultural heritage, a focus needed now more than ever to inform and to guide United States refugee policy.

This book does not pretend to provide definitive technical analyses of the demographic, political, and economic factors involved in the refugee problem or to offer legal opinions regarding the adequacy of the laws governing refugees. Nor is this a practical book on "how to help the refugees." Yet the multidimensional nature of the refugee problem requires that we touch upon its various aspects. Some basic affirmations, not meant to be platitudes, are implicit here.

(1) Although our focus is upon refugees, we recognize refugees and their problems are only one manifestation of a larger phenomenon of human dislocation related to the problems of immigrants, expatriates, repatriates, documented and undocumented aliens, and others—problems which haunt both the global and national communities. Our subject is just a segment, albeit an important segment, of a worldwide tragic phenomenon of human displacement which has become a uniquely burdensome fact of the twentieth century and which is likely to remain with us for the forseeable future.

(2) We take for granted the basic human rights of all refugees. Further, we affirm that refugees have rights as *persons*, rights which do not depend upon their legal status as citizens of the states in which they happen to reside. All religious traditions

affirm the principle of human solidarity and acknowledge that all persons, refugees included, have inalienable human rights. International law, too, gives support to the human rights of refugees, although the reality of the present world situation tends to mitigate against these rights. The way in which refugees, these most helpless of our fellow human beings, are treated is an irrefutable test of the quality of human civilization.

(3) The implementation of human rights is necessarily constrained by historical circumstances. Human rights are invariably restrained as well as protected by the state, which is expected to provide the conditions necessary for the pursuit of happiness of all its citizens, to protect individual and corporate freedom and the public welfare, to guard against crimes and disorder by means of statutory provisions, and to protect the national safety. The state also assumes as its right and duty the sole control of its borders against the entry of illegal and legal aliens, temporary visitors, and other noncitizens. It is not surprising, therefore, that the implementation of human rights, especially the human rights of refugees, is often restrained by limited resources and competing and/or conflicting claims made on the state.

(4) The state must deal with human beings within a particular national context; in principle, religion addresses itself to men and women within the context of total human existence. Religion, according to William Ernest Hocking,

> has promised to give the human individual the most complete view of his destiny and of himself. It projects that destiny beyond the range of human history. It speaks for "the whole"—a totality discernible only by thought—and a presumed ultimate source of right guidance. It provides standards of self-judgment not alone in terms of behavior, as does the law, but also in terms of motive and principle— of the inner man which the state cannot reach.[1]

Thus, although it is more easily said than done, religious men and women must acknowledge the proper duties of the state as well as legitimate religious imperatives.

(5) Without a moral consensus, the state cannot adequately exercise its obligations to create the necessary conditions for the

freedom and well-being of its citizens. Without doubt the state could use coercion to solve problems that it thought affected the common life of the community, but such coercive measures would unquestionably lack moral legitimacy. In the absence of a moral consensus, the state might easily succumb to the pressures and dictates of the currently strongest political interest group. Far better, for the state and for its citizens, is the pursuit of a policy that reflects the basic values that shape collective national life and that requires a minimum of coercion and pressure to effect and enforce. Only such a policy can inspire citizens to think, to feel, and to act for the good of the corporate life beyond the realm of their immediate needs and interests.

(6) The *religious community*—be it Jewish, Christian, Buddhist, or Islamic—is an empirical institution one step removed from "religion" as defined by Hocking. Although existing within a particular time and space, the religious community must nevertheless attempt to articulate and transmit its understanding of the truth of religion to the present generation in order to interpret—without falling into the pitfall of sectarian rhetoric—the meaning of contemporary events in light of transhistorical, transnational, and transcendental references. This understanding in turn provides the necessary motivation and the guiding principles for both private and public life. We acknowledge the difficult task of the religious community, which must both be true to its religious imperative and yet also participate fully in the corporate life of the national community without paying idolatrous veneration to the state and without becoming merely one more nongovernmental, volunteer, educational, or philanthropic organization blindly augmenting government policies and programs.

(7) Despite the principle of separation of church and state, in a democratic nation such as ours it is possible and legitimate to develop spheres of cooperation between the state and the religious community in the spirit of mutual trust and cooperation, and in mutual recognition of differences in orientation and perspective. The concern of the religious community and the concern of the state converge on many aspects of the refugee issue. Because of their humanitarian concerns and contacts both at home and abroad, religious groups have taken the initiative in

instituting a series of programs for refugees, from assisting them in finding sponsors to helping them adjust to their new environments. Such groups work in close cooperation with other voluntary groups and government agencies. The government, which has final responsibility for refugees and their problems, under heavy national and international pressure must weigh a variety of factors before making difficult decisions. Without a moral consensus, which it cannot alone create, the government cannot perform its task; and for this moral consensus it must turn to religious and other civic groups for cooperation and assistance.

\* \* \*

Recognition of the urgent need for understanding and cooperation between the government and its citizens concerning the refugee problem led the United States Coordinator for Refugee Affairs and the Religious Advisory Committee on Refugee and Migration Affairs (which includes representatives of the Jewish faith and the Roman Catholic, Anglican, Lutheran, and other Christian bodies) to cosponsor an unofficial and off-the-record conference on the ethical issues and moral principles in United States Refugee Policy. This conference convened at Meridian House International in Washington, D.C., in the spring of 1983. In a letter of invitation to members of various religious communities, the government, academia, and civic groups, H. Eugene Douglas, Ambassador-at-large and United States Coordinator for Refugee Affairs, stated:

> We live today in a world different in almost all its basic preconditions from the world of the 1880's when the Statue of Liberty was dedicated. The political and material world may well have changed, but what of the moral and ethical principles which determine how civilized men conduct their affairs—even under the most trying conditions?
>
> Each of you has been invited to this conference to examine the ethical and moral values which underpin our official refugee policy with specific reference to the pressing geopolitical realities of our time.

The conference was privileged to hear two special addresses, one by Mr. Elie Wiesel, Chairman of the United States Holocaust Memorial Council, and another by Mr. George Bush, Vice-President of the United States. The texts of their addresses are included in this volume.

The opening statements of the conference cochairmen, Richard W. Wheeler, Chairman of the Religious Advisory Committee, and Ambassador Douglas, succinctly outlined the framework of the conference. Mr. Wheeler stressed the crucial importance of moral, ethical, and religious reflection on the nature of the refugee problem in American experience, expressed in terms that can be understood throughout the world. Recognizing the fact that the issue of the refugee is inextricably intertwined with issues of the foreign and domestic policy of our own nation and of others, he asked, "How can we maintain the integrity of the status of the refugee so that that status is not only preserved, but that we, by affirming the values that are so important to all of us, can provide the aid and assistance that is [sic] desperately needed?" Mr. Wheeler also reminded the conference participants that our moral and religious responsibility must be extended not only to provide initial assistance to newly arrived refugees but also to ensure that they can soon become creative, contributing members of their new communities.

Ambassador Douglas stated his determination as United States Coordinator to work toward restoring balance, credibility, trust, and moral consensus in regard to refugee affairs and expressed the hope that the conference might achieve "not a resolution, but a strengthening of a process that will go forward in the years to come." He proposed that the conference could provide an occasion for an exchange of views on the refugee situation between religious communities and the government and assured the participants that "those of us who sit in office are not sitting and pretending to listen; we are listening." He stressed the value of American cooperation between government and nongovernmental organizations in the hope that they will work "more closely together to establish the priorities as to whom we are to help, in what order we are to help them, and what form of help to offer." He was particularly concerned with the amorphous categories of immigrant, migrant, asylee, and refugee, pointing out that confusion and ignorance make it exceedingly difficult for officials to administer laws appropriate to refugees and to provide for their care. He hoped that the conference would elicit frank, intelligent, and constructive discussion on this issue and others related to it.

*   *   *

Skeptics may question the appropriateness of such cooperation between religious groups and an agency of the government. They may suspect that the government might utilize and manipulate various religious communities in order to softsell its predetermined policies and programs. They may fear the encroachment of sectarian views into the area of national policies. It is pertinent, therefore, for us to locate the legitimate areas of mutual concern and to delineate the appropriate mode of cooperation between religious communities and the government.

In his article entitled "Caesar and the Religious Domains in America," Paul Seabury lists various models of the church-state relationship, but then states that "the missing factor in these categories, which modifies each, in providing a substance and meaning to the relationship, is the *culture within which the religious and political meet and interact*."[2] Following his observation, we might suggest that American culture has been basically religious in the broadest sense of the term, not because every citizen attends synagogue, church, or temple, but because American culture has been nurtured by the historic Jewish and Christian affirmation of the sovereignty of the Divine, of the dignity of human beings as created in God's image, and of the human responsibility to organize individual and corporate life according to the principles of love and justice.

To this end, Paul Tillich once commented that the basic thrust of Pope John XXIII's encyclical "Pacem in Terris," which stressed "the ultimate principle of justice, the acknowledgement of the dignity of every man as a person, from which follow his rights and his obligations in the manifold encounters with man," would certainly be wholeheartedly upheld by Jews, Protestants, and nonreligious humanists:

> Jews in whose prophetic tradition this principle has arisen and has been reformulated up to Martin Buber's description of the ego-thou encounter between person and person; Protestants who should never forget that the backbone of love is justice and that without the solid structure of justice, love becomes sentimentality; Humanists who have in Immanuel Kant's unconditional imperative to respect every person as person the highest criterion of *humanitas*.[3]

Indeed, these principles have become imbedded in the core of the American cultural-religious heritage as much as has the sectarian and ecclesiastical religious tradition; and they should inform, guide, and support important policies of the government as those policies are hammered out by citizens and elected officials.

Today many people—parents; teachers; religious, civic, and government leaders—lament the erosion of American culture. The buoyant optimism that characterized American culture in the past, bolstered by the abundance of material blessings which reinforced our forebears' religious vision of progress, has been severely tested in our time by domestic and global crises of great magnitude. We are beginning to understand the simple truth that culture is a very fragile "product of the human spirit, and that particular sort of product which is never finally produced; that is, culture is nothing but the *life* of human beings, and for culture to be alive means that human beings live in it."[4] It follows, then, that the task of preserving and enriching culture is not possible without the participation of human beings.

Yet we must acknowledge that even after two hundred years of democratic experiment, significant numbers among us have not had meaningful participation in common social and cultural life. The crisis of our culture today is also intensified by what John Dewey once called an "eclipse of the public" from our communities. Our society has grown too big and too fragmented, and our institutions, including the government, have become too bureaucratic and dehumanized. In such a society, a culture's coherence and cohesiveness suffer.

We must recognize that in today's cultural situation it is very difficult to pursue cogent discussions on the global problem of refugees or on American policy related to it. Assuredly many people are concerned with refugee issues—for the right or the wrong reasons. To many who are ill-informed, the refugee problem appears too huge and too complex because it is related to so many other factors: economics, politics, demography, defense, international relations, to mention only the most obvious. The problem also has fuzzy edges: it is not easy to differentiate refugees from immigrants, undocumented aliens, and other exiles. Moreover, many are overwhelmed by the enormous and never ending character of the problem. The issue looks too big for citizens or groups to deal with, and the fact that we cannot find easy resolutions makes us feel helpless and frustrated. Also, some opt to concentrate all their humanitarian sentiment and energy in assisting a few refugees with whom they come into direct contact, thus sidestepping the larger issues of global human dislocation and its policy implications for the nation.

The aim of the Conference on Ethical Issues and Moral Principles in United States Refugee Policy, which has led to this volume, was not to seek an immediate and miraculous resolution for the tangled problems of refugees. Its intent was rather to provide a public forum for mutual edification and exchange of views surrounding our national policy on this vital issue—policy which will have serious bearing on the future of our nation and the world, regardless of who occupies the White House. Those who participated in the conference represented a wide variety of political views, religious affiliations, and ethnic and cultural backgrounds; but all were united in the belief that our nation's refugee policy should reflect the shared cultural-religious values of justice, fairness, equity, and the dignity of human persons, not mere political expediency.

\* \* \*

Inasmuch as this volume came out of the Conference on Ethical Issues and Moral Principles in United States Refugee

Policy mentioned above, it is only fitting to express our indebtedness to the joint sponsors of the conference. Our special thanks go to Ambassador H. Eugene Douglas and his staff of the Office of the United States Coordinator for Refugee Affairs, especially Mrs. Jonathan Sloat (Jane), for their skill and patience in overseeing, with the officers of the Religious Advisory Committee, the entire conference. Dr. Richard Harrow Feen, Jr., Special Consultant to Ambassador Douglas' office, helped to shape the program of the conference and edited its proceedings.

Many readers may not be aware of the quiet but effective activities of the Religious Advisory Committee on Refugee and Migration Affairs and its member organizations: the American Jewish Committee, Church World Service, the United Church of Christ, the United Methodist Committee on Relief, the United Presbyterian Church in the U.S.A., the National Urban League, the Research Institute of America, the Lutheran Council in the U.S.A., the (Episcopal) Presiding Bishop's Fund for World Relief, and the United States Catholic Conference. Since its establishment in 1980, the Religious Advisory Commitee has provided counsel to the United States Coordinator for Refugee Affairs on behalf of religious institutions which have traditionally responded to the needs of refugees here and abroad. The Committee and the U.S. Coordinator work together closely on all matters concerning refugee assistance and resettlement, often in conjunction with appropriate colleagues and agencies in the private and the intergovermental sectors.

As of 1983, Religious Advisory Committee members included Mr. Richard W. Wheeler, Chairman; the Reverend Dr. August Bernthal, Vice-Chairman; the Most Reverend Anthony J. Bevilacqua; Mr. Leo Cherne; the Reverend William K. DuVal; the Reverend Dr. Harry Haines; the Reverend Dr. Paul F. McCleary; Rabbi Marc H. Tanenbaum; the Reverend Lloyd G. Van Vactor; Mr. Clarence N. Wood; the Reverend Canon Samir J. Habiby, Committee Secretariat; Mrs. Robert J. Dawson (Marion M.), Staff to the Secretariat. The Reverend John A. Huston, of the Presiding Bishop's Fund for World Relief, served as Special Assistant for the conference. We should also note that the conference and the publication of this volume were generously subsidized by the Presiding Bishop's Fund for World Relief through the good office of its Executive Director, Canon Habiby.

In addition to the conference proceedings edited by Dr. Feen, which will be made available through the Government Printing Office, the Religious Advisory Committee wishes to produce an interpretive volume that will broadly disseminate the ideas and information exchanged at the conference. Ambassador Douglas has heartily endorsed the idea and has offered the edited version of the conference proceedings, whereby the Religious Advisory Committee "will be free to include all or parts of it in any publication it may wish to issue." We greatly appreciate such a gracious gesture and have used in this volume certain portions (marked with asterisks) from the edited version of the conference proceedings. For the rest, the contributors were willing to revise their statements for this volume.

Mr. Douglas also gave us permission to include his essay, "The Problem of Refugees in a Strategic Perspective," which originally appeared in *Strategic Review* (Fall 1982, pp. 11-20). We also express our thanks to Bishop Bevilacqua for allowing us to use his "Invocation" and "Some Policy Suggestions Regarding Asylum" (originally presented as testimony to the House Subcommittee on Immigration, Refugees, and International Law in October 1981); and to the editor of *Criterion* for permission to reproduce J. M. Kitagawa's "Some Reflections on Immigration and Refugee Problems."

For the preparation of this volume, we are greatly indebted to Mrs. Marion Dawson, Assistant Director for Migration Affairs of the Presiding Bishop's Fund for World Relief, for serving as a link between the offices of Ambassador Douglas and the Religious Advisory Council, and to the Reverend Canon Charles W. Scott, then of The Seabury Press, now Executive Assistant to the Presiding Bishop, for his patience and wise counsel. We extend our thanks as well to Mr. Hermann I. Weinlick of Winston Press for his generous cooperation.

Working on this volume has been a personally gratifying experience for the editor. Although no expert on refugee affairs, he has found that his own experience of coming as a stranger to this land and of starting a new life here during a turbulent era has made him realize his obligation to share the burden of both the refugees and those who work for the cause of refugees and for a just social order. Moreover, he was able to receive sympathetic support and helpful suggestions from Dean Franklin I. Gamwell and other colleagues in the Divinity School of the University of Chicago.

Lastly, special thanks for the devotion of Mrs. Martha Morrow-Vojacek, who not only assumed the tedious editorial task but who also handled all the complicated correspondence at every stage of the editorial work. I am also indebted to my research assistant, Peter Chemery, for his help with the manuscript

J.M.K.

*Notes*

1. William Ernest Hocking, *The Coming World Civilization* (New York, 1956), p. 47.
2. Paul Seabury, "Caesar and the Religious Domain in America," *Teaching Political Science* 10, no. 1 (Fall 1982): 22. (Italics mine.)
3. Paul Tillich, "Pacem in Terris," *Criterion* (Spring 1965), p. 15.
4. William Earle, *Public Sorrows and Private Pleasures* (Bloomington, Indiana, 1976), p. 75.

# *Addresses*

# Who Is a Refugee?*

## Elie Wiesel

I remember, after the war in Europe, the preoccupation we had with the Jewish saying "What are we to do with strangers?" Therefore, I think that what you are doing here is of extreme importance. It is almost condescending to say it because you know it. A civilization can be measured by its attitude towards strangers. We have witnessed in this century a new category of stranger—the refugee. And it is, therefore, on that subject I will try to say a few words.

I remember an anecdote I heard in Paris after the war. The anecdote is about two refugees in Marseilles during the occupation. They met simply because they would come day after day and stand in line before consulates where Gian-Carlo Menotti's consul played God. They could not get visas. It took them days and weeks. They would go to all the consulates available and could not get visas. Finally, they did. One man said to the other, "Where are you going?"

He said, "I am going to South Africa. And you?" The first replied, "I am going to Tierra del Fuego." "That is far," he said. And the other said, "Far from where?"

This anecdote describes, I believe, the situation both psychological and philosophical of the refugee. Everything suddenly changes. All the notions and all the concepts have been altered, even geography. Suddenly, the street you are on is a different universe. Suddenly, the house you are in is a different world. What you are trying to do here—I hope it is what we are trying to do—is to offer a shorter distance to people who feel as strangers in the world.

When did I become a refugee? After all, I imagine that is why you invited me here tonight. When was it? Was it when I was still in my town, 1944, and the last Jewish families of my town were led into the courtyard of the last synagogue? I was very young. We did not know anything. We only knew there was a war going on. We also knew that the war would be ended soon, but we did not know anything of the other side, of the Kingdom of the Darkness that existed somewhere, so near and yet so far.

We thought, people then in Hungary, that we would not leave Hungary because Hungary would protect its citizens. Then we came to a table where the Hungarian gendarmes simply took the papers that we handed them. When my turn came, as anybody else's, to give my citizenship papers, he did not even look into them. He simply tore them up. That is what he did with all the papers. Is it then that I became a refugee?

Suddenly, I felt that my town was no longer my town, my home was no longer my home, and the people with whom I had lived for so many years were no longer neighbors, but enemies.

Did I become a refugee later when I joined a different category of people, a category of people who suddenly have no name, no face, almost no destiny—forsaken, forgotten, forlorn, abandoned by God and man alike?

Is it later when I came to Paris? I do not know why; simply I had nowhere else to go. Together with 400 other children, Jewish children from Buchenwald, we came to Paris. Stateless. No connection. All we knew was that we knew too much. Then we became nominally, legally refugees. But when did it begin?

Strange. You should know that while I was in Paris there were refugees from Germany and Austria and Italy who had a different name. They were called then "displaced persons." I was wondering before, why was the word suddenly taken away? Why was I looking for the word?

As I was doing some research on the refugee experience, trying to bring you something that you know in my own words, I found out that there are many people who have left their countries and who deserve our sympathy, our help, our generosity, and also our humanity. Yet, they are not all alike.

What are we to do with people who could live where they are living except they prefer a better homeland, better economic conditons? They should be helped. We should help everybody. But are they on the same level, in the same category, as people who need to be with us because, if not, they would die or lose their freedom? Which means, is an expatriate equal to a refugee? Is a migrant equal to a refugee? Is an immigrant equal to a refugee?

Now, all are strangers. Strangely enough, the only category that has a certain positive element in the word is that of refugee—because it has refuge. Yet, he is the most tragic of all, he or she. There was one category lost, however: that of displaced persons, as they were called in 1945 to 1950. I am trying to understand, why did we forget this term? Perhaps because we were ashamed of it.

On the one hand, perhaps there was a certain desire to humanize the term. What other word could we find for people who lived in camps in Germany and Austria near the very camps where they had lost all they had? I am convinced that the urge not to face their suffering is what motivated the very neutral, beautiful word "displaced person." It is a poetic sense that propagated that word.

What we are doing even today is a result of what happened then, a change of language. As a teacher, as a writer, of course, I deal with language. Suddenly, I realize what is happening to our language, what we are doing to our language. Have you noticed that there are no more "poor people," only "developing nations"? Have you noticed that there are no more "revolutions," but "destabilizations" in certain countries? Have you noticed that governments no longer "lie"? They simply "indulge in disinformation."

The same thing, I am sure, happened then, too. Every one of these persons had seen deaths more than once, had seen humanity at its lowest stage. Whatever that person had seen, no university will ever teach or learn. Yet, we gave them a name, "displaced person," as though a cataclysm had come, a kind of earthquake. As if they had had to leave because of too much rain. We forgot the human element there. They were victims of the human system, of a human-inhuman system.

Who is a refugee? What is a refugee? Simply because a person left a country, even if he had to leave the country, is he a refugee?

Forgive me for this example—it is an extreme example that I will use to illustrate a middle. What about those trapped in jail—

or worse places? Shouldn't they be accepted somewhere? Don't they deserve to have refuge somewhere?

No. I think they are fugitives; I think they are criminals. I think refugees are only those who are victims. A refugee is by definition a victim, although in the beginning there was a certain privilege attached to that status. Think of the great refugees—Thomas Mann, Franz Werfel, Stefan Zweig, or Joseph Roth—they lived in Paris in their cafes, and yet they wrote. And what they did write, we teach today. There was a certain honor attached to the name. To be a refugee from Nazi Germany or Communist Stalinist Russia was an honor, a privilege. It still is.

So, what is a refugee? Only someone who is a victim of an oppressive, inhuman society and, therefore, deserves our respect and perhaps our gratitude—surely our compassion.

Think of a refugee. Here is a man or woman or a child who arrives in a new place where he inspires suspicion. Strangers inspire suspicion and fear. So, these poor people who needed someone did not get accepted. They lived among themselves. In Paris, they were called the émigré circles. In Los Angeles, where they lived during the war, too, they lived among themselves. Somehow they were not adopted. They were not accepted by the general society. Why not?

Imagine a refugee who comes to a new country where he has no friends, where everything is a burden. His language is a burden. Now what would a writer do without his language? Suddenly, Thomas Mann has no language because he is luckily accepted in a new country which gives him refuge, but he remains a refugee. It means being a refugee may be a metaphysical condition, then, not only a political situation.

Strange again—when these people come into a new country, they will tell you that the food tastes different. The apple does not have the same taste here as it had in Thailand or in Hungary. In the new country everything is different—its geography, its science, its morality or certain concepts of morality. It is then that any refugee whom we confront becomes our judge. He passes judgment on our values, on our society.

What are we doing with our culture? What we are doing with it, you know, is no good. I am sure you share my outrage. I think never have chaos and confusion reigned so totally over the world. Scientifically, we go very far. We know the other side of the moon, but we forgot to look into the heart of our neighbor. Do we really know what hurts the other person, the stranger? Do we care to know?

Last week, I was thinking about it. I was on a Concorde jet from London. I thought to myself, when I was young, when I was my students' age or younger and had to go and see my grandfather, who lived seven kilometers from my town, I was still using a horse and carriage. So, in my lifetime we made that jump from horse and carriage to Concorde and lasers and Star Wars.

Technologically, we make progress; no doubt about it. It is extraordinary. It is beautiful, what we can do. But think what we could do if every school of engineering, every school of medicine could have compulsory courses in ethics and the humanities. It is the most important issue that faces us and the future, if there is a future: ethics. What are we to do with our knowledge? The refugee, when he looks at us, is asking us, is questioning us, on that. What are you doing with my knowledge that I brought you?

Now those who come are lucky; many aren't. My friends, I cannot tell you how grateful I am to be in this country. I rarely say it because it is obvious. I came here a stateless person. I am even an ardent supporter and admirer, believe it or not, of the American bureaucracy. Let me tell you why.

After I went to France, I was in Paris working as a journalist and my newspaper sent me to New York. I did not have a passport, I had a kind of travel document. I came here with a journalistic visa to the United Nations.

After a few weeks in New York, a taxi ran over me and I had to spend a whole year in the hospital, in and out, a whole year on crutches, and so forth. Suddenly, I realized my visa was up, and I went to the immigration office. They said my document was valid for only one year. I went back to the French consulate and they said I had to go back to France because refugees' documents can only be renewed in France. I went back to the immigration office and they said, "What can we do?" I said, "What can I do? I'm in a wheelchair."

I went back and forth, back and forth, to consulate and immigration, until someone in immigration said to me, "Why don't you become an American?" I said, "Do you think I can?" He said, "Many have." "How does one do it?" I asked. He gave me the forms and so forth. And that is how I became an American.

But from 1940 to 1945, when the Nazis had the power of life and death, even this country did not do its duty. It hurts me to this day that hundreds and thousands of people could have—with one piece of paper, with one signature, with one letter, with one telegram—remained alive. That telegram was not sent, and that piece of paper was not given. Why not? The quotas were not even exhausted.

Thus, there were refugees in France waiting in line, and some committed suicide because they could not wait any longer. The most tragic case is Walter Benjamin, the great philosopher. Walter Benjamin was in France and had the offer to go to Spain, but they closed the borders. He saw they would send him back. He committed suicide. How many—especially intellectuals—committed suicide? How many people felt they could not take it any longer only because the gates of this nation were also closed?

This country, after all, was built for refugees: not only by, but for. When Christopher Columbus left Spain, it was, in the Jewish calendar, the ninth day of Ab, 1492. On that day we commemorate the destruction of our Temple. It is the most tragic day of the year. That day in 1492 was also the last day for the Jews to leave Spain. When Christopher Columbus went aboard, he met the last Jews leaving Spain. I think there are no accidents in history. There is something to this event. I think he went on his mission to open a new haven, a new refuge for more and more refugees.

I know the problems in helping these refugees are difficult. I know they were difficult then, too, with the war going on. But still, the question must be asked—it is tormenting me—"What can be done now?" I don't know, of course. There are legal problems, provocative problems, and you are better at understanding them than I. But may I give you one naive proposal? Why not bring in all the orphans, all the refugee orphans, real refugee orphans? Otherwise, you would say, how can you separate the children from the parents? Don't. But the orphans, bring them here—all the forlorn souls who need a home. They deserve one gesture of kindness somewhere. Let us open our hearts for them.

We have all had suffering. But have we all learned something from suffering? What to do with it? I went back to the Bible. I always go back to the Bible when I have a problem. I wanted to know who was the first refugee in the world. First I thought it was Moses. After all, he was the one who fled oppression. He went to Midian because he fled from Pharaoh's police. Like all refugees, he gave back a contribution to society.

Then I thought it was Jeremiah perhaps. The refugee par excellence, who was a refugee everywhere, even in his country. Then I thought, no, perhaps it was Joseph. There was a time when I called Joseph the first Kissinger of history. Then I came back to Adam. Whom did he flee? Whom did he escape from? God. How do I know he was a refugee? Because at one point, you remember, we are told that God turned to Adam and said, "Where are you?" There was a great Hasidic master who asked a marvelous question. He said, "Is it conceivable, is it possible, that God did not know where Adam was?" The answer is God knew; Adam did not. My question is "Do we?"

# Remarks on United States Refugee Policy

## George Bush

It is a great pleasure to be with such a distinguished group of leaders dedicated to the important and moving work of refugee relief. Many of you here today have made significant contributions to this great humanitarian effort and will, I am sure, continue to make many more.

Refugee relief is a subject that touches me personally very deeply. In the past two years, I have talked with the leaders of key international organizations—the United Nations High Commissioner for Refugees Paul Hartling and President of the International Red Cross Alexandre Hay. In these conversations I have stressed, as I will stress to you today, the United States' continuing commitment to lending the fullest possible support to the great effort of international refugee assistance.

During my trip to Africa last fall, I was deeply impressed by the hospitality and generosity that many African countries show toward refugees—in spite of the severe economic hardships in those countries. It gave me great pride that our country had made a major and early pledge of assistance to African refugees at the 1981 International Conference on African Refugees. On my trip, we saw that assistance at work.

One of our country's finest traditions is the help and haven given to refugees throughout the world. We are ourselves a nation of immigrants and are all the richer for it. Our tradition of refugee assistance reflects deep principles and abiding commitments, and we can be proud of our record. For example:

• Since 1975 more than 750,000 Indochinese refugees have been successfully resettled in the United States. That is the largest single influx of people into our country in this century, and it has been accomplished despite marked economic problems and cultural differences.

- We have recently overcome barriers to the immigration of Amerasian children and their mothers from Vietnam to the United States.
- All in all, we have accepted more refugees than all other resettlement countries combined.
- Since 1979 alone, we have spent more than one billion dollars for worldwide refugee relief assistance, working directly with concerned countries and through many international and private organizations, including those represented here today. And this sum does not include our major expenditures for resettlement in the United States.
- We have led the international community in responding to relief needs in Cambodia and Africa, and in support of the nearly 3 million Afghan refugees in Pakistan.

Added to the federal efforts are the extraordinary contributions, in time and money, by the American people and organizations in the private sector. The partnership between our private and public efforts in this area is unique and critical. It is the key to our success, and I know our Coordinator, Gene Douglas, will continue to give high priority to enhancing that partnership and the effectiveness of our programs.

We cannot, of course, afford to rest on America's record. Enormous tasks remain in Indochina, Africa, South Asia and elsewhere. Many challenges, old and new, need to be met. We need to give, and we are giving, additional attention to meeting the special needs of women and children, who constitute the majority of refugees. We are also working to eliminate the revolting piracy of boat people in Southeast Asian waters which sorely magnifies the human suffering of those refugees.

The tasks of resettlement at home will also continue to challenge us. For this reason, we have undertaken new programs to increase the refugees' chances of successfully integrating into our society.

Our strong commitment to helping refugees is reflected in President Reagan's 1981 statement on immigration and refugees. He stressed that "we shall continue America's tradition as a land that welcomes peoples from other countries" and that we shall also "continue to share in the responsibility of welcoming and resettling those who flee oppression."

As we do so, however, we should never lose sight of the fact that refugees are a result of a much larger problem in this world.

Back in 1951, the United Nations High Commission was founded as a *temporary* institution to deal with the 6 million refugees in the wake of World War II. Over thirty years and many billions of dollars later, we have more refugees in the world today than ever before. Why?

I think we have to face squarely the root causes of the refugee problem. These causes are as old as a society itself—war, repression or persecution, and civil strife. These sources of instability are sometimes caused by indigenous factors and internal problems. But all too often such instability is instigated and exacerbated by external forces—in this century, most often by the Soviet Union, its sympathizers, or its clients.

Peoples from many countries are being forced to flee their homes. Most are coming from such places as Afghanistan, Ethiopia, Vietnam, Laos, and Cambodia—not to mention Cuba and Nicaragua. There were no South Vietnamese boat people before that country was overrun. Nearer to us, we are witnessing the disruption of societies in Central America and the Caribbean, encouraged and abetted by the Soviet Union, Cuba, and Nicaragua.

The refugee problem is therefore bound up with the broader purposes of our country's foreign and security policies. The Reagan administration is strongly committed to advancing the causes of freedom and pluralism; to improving human rights conditions and alleviating the economic problems that give rise to instability; to resisting the expansion and influence of totalitarian ideologies in whatever guises. The administration's policies and programs—both foreign policy and our defense effort—are directed at the basic problems of international instability which give rise, among other things, to refugees.

We need to continue to help refugees as well as we can throughout the world. But the goal is not just to help refugees, but to alter those circumstances that give rise to persecution and force people to flee their homes. Ultimately, our success will be measured by our ability to advance those ideals and principles that are at the heart of American and other democratic societies. That moral responsibility rests on all of us.

I congratulate you for your efforts on these humanitarian issues, and I wish you every success in the days ahead as we work together on the urgent problem of refugee relief.

# Dimensions of the Refugee Problem: Three Panel Discussions

# I. Refugees in the Contemporary World Scene

Throughout the ages victims of natural calamities, warfare, and political change have come to be known as "refugees." Into this category have fallen as well ethnic, cultural, political, or religious groups expelled from their homelands by hostile rulers or majority groups. Some of these refugees have been able eventually to return to their homelands; others have been destined to resettle elsewhere. For the most part, the problems of the refugees have been handled locally, regionally, or nationally on an *ad hoc* basis. In the past, national borders were less rigidly controlled than they are today, and movement of all peoples, refugees included, across borders was more easily accomplished. Since the nineteenth century, however, sovereign nations have begun to tighten border control of citizens, especially refugees, of other countries. Movement of refugees in the twentieth century has become even more difficult as national sovereignty has become more rigidly defined and as social, economic, and political upheavals, as well as interstate conflicts and large-scale wars, have created refugees and other displaced persons in numbers heretofore unknown.

Although our primary concern is ethical and moral principles involved in United States refugee policy, our reflection must take into account at least three indisputable realities: First, the refugee problem within our national borders is only a part of a larger global problem. Second, we must be sensitive not only to the political and economic realities that cause and influence refugee flow but also to the more basic issue of human rights and the theoretical and practical implications involved therein. Third, all nations, not least ourselves, lack unlimited resources to meet the legitimate needs of all refugees and thus are compelled to make difficult choices on levels of both policy and practical implementation. There is no simple policy which will do even minimal justice to the multitude who justly claim a "well-founded fear of persecution" today. A few decades ago, the ethical and moral issues concerning refugees from the Nazis or from the Soviet Union were more clear-cut. Now, however, increasing numbers of refugees from Asia, Africa, and Latin America pose a more complex series of ethical and moral issues that are more ambiguous.

The following reflections were presented at the first panel, moderated by President John Silber of Boston University, at the aforementioned conference on Ethical Issues and Moral Principles in United States Refugee Policy. There were no consultations among the panel members prior to the conference. The spoken style of each presenter has been preserved. Brief biographical sketches of the moderators and presenters of all three panels appear in appendices.

# *Introduction*

## John R. Silber

In my remarks setting the stage for this first panel I want to address what I consider to be some of the central ethical and moral principles of U.S. refugee policy.

Last night, you recall, Elie Wiesel identified Adam as the first refugee, and this morning Bishop Bevilacqua reminded us in his moving invocation that as sons and daughters of Adam we are all refugees. That places the issue in a theological perspective, giving us identity with the subjects we are discussing.

Our review last night of the concept "refugee" was remarkably constructive and prepared us well for the discussion today. The refugee, Mr. Wiesel pointed out, is a victim. The refugee, he said, takes refuge. That of course is true, but it is not an adequate definition because it is too inclusive: there are victims who are never refugees, for example, persons starving in Ethiopia and other countries of Africa who are not trying to go anywhere. They are victims but not refugees. We have to understand what we mean by taking refuge. What is this act of taking refuge that defines one as a refugee?

Wiesel remarked on the important distinction between refugee and displaced person, and wondered why the useful term "displaced person" had largely fallen from the vocabulary. The term itself contains a very important clue: that the person has been displaced, has been driven out. This would indicate that there is more than one kind of refugee: the refugee who is driven out and the refugee who makes a decision to become a wanderer.

Those who leave voluntarily, as Mr. Wiesel reminded us last night, need not be refugees. Some may be emigrants from one country and immigrants to another. Those of us here who are not themselves immigrants to the United States are all the descendants of emigrants from other countries. And many of us here are children of persons who emigrated from other countries.

My father, for example, was an emigrant, but in no sense a refugee. He came to what he thought of as a land of a thousand possibilities. It was the land of opportunity for most of the persons coming to the United States. Whether any individual was a refugee or an emigrant depends on the intensity of need from which they were moving. An Irishman who in 1847 faced a clear choice between emigration or starvation was a refugee. But the graduate of an architectural school in Germany who came to the United States to improve his chances was only an emigrant. Between the two extremes most cases can be ranked on a sliding scale.

One of the most interesting things that Mr. Wiesel said last night was that among our immigrants are also fugitives, and fugitives are surely not refugees. The Nazis who went to Latin America may have been displaced persons, if one does not think of displaced persons as persons who are worthy. But they were literally fugitives from justice.

That means that fugitives have to be examined very carefully. Are some fugitives to be recognized and given refugee status? We should explore this issue because some fugitives claim that they are guilty merely of political crimes; it is very important for us to understand what we mean by political crimes.

It has become common in the United States in the last fifteen years to hear it argued that anything done for a political purpose is a political crime. The Weathermen, when they blew up the graduate student at the University of Wisconsin, were engaging in a criminal activity for a political purpose. But it degrades language and thought alike to call such an act a political crime. A political crime is an act that is made criminal solely because of its political content. Bonhoeffer undoubtedly was put in prison and suffered because of acts that were merely political: no crimes at all, simply the expression of free thought, an action that any decent man would take. But those who murder with a political motive are not political criminals unless we wish to extend that status to Adolf Hitler and Joseph Stalin, consummate criminals whose ends were entirely political. Unless we define political crime very carefully, we will fall into a bog that we will have difficulty in getting out of, particularly when we address the issue of asylum.

This morning television carried a report of a local case in which unidentified—and shrouded—persons alleged to be refugees from El Salvador are taking "asylum" in a church.

I would hope that the churchmen present today can assist us to clarify the concept of asylum. In the last days of the Vietnam conflict, the School of Theology at Boston University frequently invoked the concept of asylum. When an AWOL Marine hid himself in our chapel, some of the faculty announced that he had sought sanctuary. But surely a theological faculty would know that the concept of sanctuary was developed in the middle ages, when the church was established, with a clearly understood temporal power that existed side by side with that of the king. The contemporary Methodist Church—or Boston University—has no equivalent independence from secular society. Moreover, the medieval concept of sanctuary required the person seeking it, in the phrase of the time, "to abjure the realm." He forfeited all his civil rights and his property, and became in effect the serf of the lord who granted him sanctuary. Sanctuary was not a temporary status but a permanent one, embodying all of the temporal disadvantages of the monastic life and none of the spiritual advantages. In the rare cases when someone took sanctuary only temporarily, it was because he had been able to compose the quarrel with the government which had led to his taking sanctuary in the first place.

Sanctuary as proposed in the situation at Boston University was essentially a publicity stunt, and it utterly degraded the concept of asylum. It stripped the church of much of its dignity and, more important, all of its integrity—at least in the eyes of ordinary Americans able to read and write.

The refugee, in contrast to the fugitive, is essentially innocent. Not necessarily in the eyes of God, but innocent before the laws of man: an innocent person who either is driven from his home or, because of varying degrees of suffering or oppression, voluntarily moves from one place to another. It is essential for us to understand that there are degrees of voluntary action and to establish scales for distinguishing the refugee from the emigrant. In short, how extreme must the provocation be before the emigrant takes on the status of the refugee?

These are some of the problems that we have to face, elucidated to a large extent by our discussion last night. But as we face these problems, I want to ask the panel to review them according to certain fundamental principles which, if accepted, might provide useful guidance for all of our discussion. One of these concerns the question whether we as a nation and as a people have finite responsibilities or whether we have obligations only the Almighty can meet.

One may commit the sin of pride by supposing that he has moral responsibilities substantially in excess of his capacity. If I am right, we are not obligated to take on infinite responsibilities and to try actually to do the impossible; our finite capacities restrict our obligations to finite dimensions. It follows that there is validity in viewing the problem of refugees in the context of a balance between productivity and consumption.

If the world cannot consume more than the world produces, and if we continue to export Western technology and medicine, which increase the world's population without exporting an adequate understanding of population control and the means to achieve it, we will never be able to solve the refugee problem. If we are not more thoughtful and responsible, we will eventually create a refugee problem of a proportion so vast that it can be solved only by one or more of the terrible horses of the Apocalypse—the most terrible of which in a world of nuclear weapons is war.

# Tragic Choices in Refugee Policy

## Michael S. Teitelbaum

Our purpose is to discuss refugee policy in ethical and moral terms. You may ask, why now? There is nothing new about refugees—they go right back to the Garden of Eden. And ethical and moral concerns are certainly not new.

What is new, I think, is our recognition that today's refugee movements pose ethical and moral choices that are *tragic*— choices that *all* of us would prefer to avoid, but that we can avoid no longer. These tragic choices are before us because of a new reality and new knowledge about reality. The new reality is that refugee movements are no longer temporary, episodic crises of manageable proportions, as was the Hungarian crisis of 1956. They seem now to be continuous and of very large size. The new knowledge comes from modern communications: we can no longer be blissfully ignorant of the suffering of millions of refugees in remote places. Thirty years ago very few of us would ever have known about the Indochinese boat people.

In their book entitled *Tragic Choices*, Bobbit and Calabresi tell us that a tragic choice is one which brings into conflict the ultimate values by which society defines itself. It may be true that societies are forced to mask tragic choices in order to preserve their moral foundation. *Nevertheless, choices must still be made.* Some choices, I would argue, are better than others. My goal is to sketch the contours of these tragic choices, and to suggest some guidelines we might use in making such choices. As I see it, refugee and asylum policy presents us with no fewer than *four* tragic choices:

(1) The first tragic choice is *definitional*. The definition of refugee under international law makes some fairly clear distinctions between who *is* and who *is not* a refugee: only those who

have left their country owing to a well-founded fear of *persecution* for reasons of race, religion, nationality, membership in a particular social group, or political opinion are considered refugees. This definition *excludes* tens of millions of equally desperate people fleeing the random and general violence of a civil or an international war; people starving in a desperately poor country; or people fleeing the aftermath of a natural disaster such as an earthquake or a drought. Groups such as the Organization for African Unity, who argue for a broadened definition to include other categories of desperate people, have a strong ethical case. But they must confront the first tragic choice: if the definition is indeed broadened, we qualify and raise the hopes of millions of people—but we still lack the means (or the will) to provide desirable solutions for them.

(2) Then, regardless of whether the definition is expanded, the question remains *to whom* to provide permanent refuge. This is tragic choice number two. The facts are sobering:

*Fact #1:* The Refugee Act of 1980 contemplated a "normal flow" of 50,000 refugees per year until this year. The number is now set by consultation between Congress and the president.

*Fact #2:* "Guesstimates" of the number of refugees in the world begin at eight million and work up from there, even under the unexpanded definition.

So tragic choice number two is how to allocate 50,000—or even 200,000 or 500,000—slots among 8 million deserving people.

(3) The third tragic choice involves *resources*. The UNHCR terms three outcomes as "durable solutions" to a refugee's plight. In order of desirability, these are first, repatriation; second, first country asylum; and third, permanent resettlement in a third country. According to the Refugee Coordinator's calculations, in fiscal year 1982 the United States spent approximately $2,315,000,000 on refugees and "entrants"; three-fourths or more of this amount went to finance the domestic resettlement of fewer than one million persons since 1975, while the remaining one-fourth went to the *many* millions of others *not* resettled. Of course, more than $ 2.3 billion could be allocated, or benefits to each resettled refugee could be reduced, or fewer could be resettled and more assistance provided to refugees in

countries of first asylum. Hence tragic choice number three is posed by a limited supply of resettlement slots and other resources in the context of virtually unlimited demand.

We have thus come full circle to the central tragic choice of who: whom shall we admit, and based on what criteria? Should we favor the young? The old? The skilled? Those with relatives here? The most desperate (and who are they)? The most deserving (and who are they)? Should there be equality by country? By region? By social class? By race? And what is equality? Equal numbers? Equal percentages? What about the provision in the 1980 Refugee Act singling out those of "special humanitarian concern to the United States"? And finally, how about asylees? What is the ethical justification for granting them permanent residence when they have, in effect, jumped the queue of worthy seekers of refuge?

(4) The fourth tragic choice comes from what bankers call a "moral hazard" (insurance may encourage risk-taking)—the apparent reality that explicit or implicit *promise of admission as refugees stimulates its own refugee flows*. We have seen this phenomenon in the Cuban case: a statement such as President Carter's "open arms and an open heart" may make all of us feel better, but it also stimulated tens of thousands of additional Cubans to head for Mariel Harbor. UNHCR staff members and others have alleged that this country's open-ended and generous Indochinese refugee settlement policy stimulated movement to the boats. (Some have even stated that the goal of U.S. refugee policy was to destabliize Vietnam.) The failure to deal promptly with Haitian asylum claims sent the message back to Haiti that "if only you can get to Florida, they will let you stay and find a high-wage job." This led ultimately to the Krome North detention camps so widely criticized. And who knows how many people died in the boats that headed out to sea as a result? How many of us bear some unintended responsibility for these deaths?

Some of us might argue that refugee and asylee decisions need not be reduced to tragic choices. After all, only certain tragic choices arise from natural scarcity; most arise from conscious political decisions among trade-offs. And, indeed, it is tempting to us to duck the tragic choice (or to imagine that we can do so) by arguing for much larger refugee admissions. But the choices cannot be ducked, since no one contemplates numbers large enough to make the tragic choices unnecessary.

Moreover, as Ambassador Douglas noted, in the real world refugee admissions *will* be limited through the political process. The question is whether a generous refugee policy can sustain broad public support. Ironically, advocates of unlimited or greatly expanded refugee or asylum admissions may be the worst threat to a generous policy. In short, as in many other areas, *the perfect can be the enemy of the good*.

A final issue relates to the question of *temporary* refuge—that is, asylum or extended voluntary departure applicants. Unfortunately, United States policy might be summed up by the following perverse irony: *our humanity has made us inhumane*. It may be that the United States has been strict in granting temporary refuge because of a "well-founded fear" that in the American political and judicial systems, temporary refuge will become a *permanent* residence. In addition, the use of refugee *camps* for temporary refuge—as in most other countries of first asylum—would surely be criticized by many of us. Imagine temporary refuge camps for Salvadorans along the United States-Mexican border. What would we call them? Prisons? "Concentration camps"? So the United States practice is to deny asylum claims by many Salvadorans but to wink at their illegal entry.

Having left you with these dilemmas to contemplate, I wish to close with a modest warning: a manipulated or an incompetent refugee/asylee policy is an ethically dangerous game. To use refugee/asylee admissions as "hostile acts" aimed at foreign adversaries—as the United States has done—makes it far more difficult to admit bona fide refugees from friendly nations, as amply demonstrated during the Cuban-Haitian migrations of 1980. To assuage one's conscience by focusing upon United States resettlement of a small proportion of the world's refugees, while the majority go begging, is an understandable effort to avoid a tragic choice that is unavoidable. Unwillingness to defend the integrity of the refugee concept is ethically questionable. To guarantee admission to a high-wage economy to successful boat people is an invitation to them to risk their lives in boats.

The philosopher Stuart Hampshire has written that "for the tragic consciousness, a strong will to put things right will end in mistake and self-destruction, because the sources of wrong are always too remote, and beyond the reach of any solitary virtue." This is not prescription for inaction—but it argues for the realism and balance that a generous and sustainable refugee policy requires.

# Who Is a Refugee?
## Distinction Between Economic and Political Determinants of Refugee Movements

### Anthony J. Bevilacqua

The word "refugee" is derived from the Latin word, *refugium*, meaning a shelter, security, a haven. A refugee, therefore, in the derivative sense of the term, is one who seeks a shelter, security, a haven. This is an inalienable right that belongs to every human being by the very fact that he or she is a person endowed by God with certain rights. Among the most basic rights inherent in the very nature of man as a person is the right to have available all of the means to achieve here on earth fullness as a creature of God and to achieve eternal happiness as a child of God in heaven.

Recent years, particularly since the horrible cruelties that the Vietnamese boat people suffered in 1977-78 and that the media vividly portrayed to us, have demonstrated that refugee movements no longer seem to be temporary crises but are a permanent reality of humanity—or rather of inhumanity. An impression is growing into an awareness that every day and everywhere refugees are with us and will be with us.

This permanence of refugee movements and the vastness of the numbers present a serious problem, physical and moral, to the international community. Whether we want to be or not, whether we like it or not, we are members of one human family created by God and, therefore, our concern for those in need, both in feelings and in action, must transcend national boundaries and legal barriers to the extent that it is productive. We are our brother's keeper. As Dr. Charles Keely stated, "Refugees are not subordinate to the interests of global politics. Man is the measure of societies and of governments and of their policies. It is not the other way around."

The definition of refugee so frequently determines the responsibility and the reaction of the international community. The definition of refugee is not a self-evident one to governments. It is government which designates the criteria or the notion of refugee. In other words, the criteria are basically social designations.

The definition of refugee best known is that taken from the 1951 "Convention Relating to the Status of Refugees" and the "Protocol of 1967 Related to the General Assembly Declaration on Asylum." About seventy-eight countries have signed these documents. The United Nations defines a refugee as a person who, owing to well-grounded fear of being persecuted for reasons of race, religion, nationality, membership in a particular social group, or political opinion, is outside the country of his nationality and is unable or, owing to such fear, is unwilling to avail himself of the protection of that country.

From the above definition, we can immediately see why there is so much confusion regarding the meaning of refugee. The United Nations' definition attempts to restrict the notion of refugee to political determinants of flight and would exclude from the status of refugee economic determinants or internal displacement even for political repression.

The United Nations' definition requires the suffering persecuted person to be outside his national boundaries because the international community is hesitant to intervene in internal matters. One must recall that the legal concept of refugee arose largely after World War I when there were so many displaced, undocumented persons outside their own nation and the international community felt that it had to assume the responsibility for them. This reflects a serious inadequacy with the United Nations' definition, since the international community does not feel it has any responsibility over displaced persons within a nation no matter how horrendous the persecution, no matter how vast the suffering, no matter how fatal the economic deprivation. We have here an illustration of the conflict between the human and the legal use of the designation "refugee." The United Nations limits the status of refugee to political persecution for the five reasons of race, religion, nationality, social group, political opinion. This does not mean to deny the suffering from other factors (e.g., economic or civil strife) nor to reject a call to the international community for aid. Rather it is an attempt to specify carefully the elements of the definition so as to identify clearly the politically persecuted as a category for which the international community can assume responsibility.

It is proper to ask here how one can distinguish migrants for economic reasons from political refugees. The answer is important because many will say that to equate political and economic refugees would qualify enormous numbers of people to claim refugee status if they could manage to flee their own country. Persecution, however, is often a relative term. In many areas, people are repressed and are in danger because of civil strife, public disorder, economic deprivation. In fact, government (e.g., Vietnam) will resort to harsh economic restrictions as an instrument of deprivation compelling the person to flee.

As was stated above, the definition of refugee is a social creation which developed after World War I as a result of the flight of peoples from developed European countries. In recent years, the causes of refugee movements are different. Most flow from the third world developing or new nations. What can we do with this new reality of vast numbers of displaced persons? Some would change the definition of refugee or at least develop a new and broader interpretation of it. Others would say that nothing is gained by changing the definition so that it would include all categories of those in need, such as economic refugees.

It would be more realistic and helpful for the international community to extend its responsibility to all of the other categories of people who are displaced by economic deprivation, civil strife, natural disasters. This international responsibility to these displaced victims should be seen as an obligation of the international community for the very purpose of preserving and developing the welfare, peace, and stability of the international community. In other words, nations today must look not only to their own national common good but also to the common good of the human family, that is, to the international common good.

In the midst of the debate on the notion of refugee, we must remember that it remains the obligation of everyone to assist all people in need. If I may be permitted to paraphrase an old maxim, "I would rather help a refugee than know how to define one."

# Humanitarian Proclivities
## and the Pressure of Politics

## Peter I. Rose

Few photographs are more heartrending than the classic Madonna shot of the thin refugee mother and her dull-eyed baby. It is a familiar portrait used by government agencies, the news media, and social service organizations to bring to public attention the private suffering of thousands of human beings caught up in the cross currents of revolution or the aftermath of war. In recent years the Madonna of the refugee camps has tended to have an Asian visage. She is usually Vietnamese, or a person who escaped from Cambodia. She could, as well, be Chinese, or Lao, or Hmong, of Afghan, or Ethiopian, Haitian, or Palestinian. Her specific ethnicity is less important to the viewer than her condition, for she is a symbol. With silent eloquence she communicates and is intended to communicate the pathos of being uprooted, alienated, and afraid.

Despite their apotheosis, not all refugees are saints. But most do share common characteristics. In law, as we have heard, they are victims of persecution who were forced, for political reasons, to flee their homelands. In fact, they are more than victims, they are dependents. And therein lies much of our problem. For refugees are people dependent on others to rescue them from their plight. They need others to provide them with assistance to meet immediate physical needs, and to aid them in making some sort of new life in a neighboring land, or in a third country, once the initial trauma of escape has been dealt with.

As Bruce Grant, author of *The Boat People*, has explained, this state of dependence means that refugees often share another fate. Despite the moving portrait that elicits compassion, for many in the receiving societies, and I quote, the refugee is an unwanted person. He or she makes a claim upon the humanity of others without having much to give in return. If after resettlement a refugee works hard or is lucky, or is successful, he may be accused of taking the work of someone else. If he fails, he is thought to be ungrateful and a burden on the community.

A refugee is especially unwanted by officials. His papers are rarely in order, his health is often suspect, and sometimes, although he claims to be fleeing from persecution, he is thought of as simply trying to get from one poor overpopulated land to a rich underpopulated one.

Like Camus' stranger, the refugee is almost invariably a person apart, an outsider who peers into closed rooms. He seeks admittance but is never sure of his acceptability. Friends tell him he must not look back, but in his heart he can hear what the Russian exiles call "the evening bells of home." He is caught in limbo, in a paradoxical state of permanent instability.

To be sure, as John Silber suggested, not all refugees are equally poor or equally alienated. Some have easier times than others. It is the case, I think, that those who are socially, religiously, or politically marginal prior to their exile (i.e., those who are members of what we now call minority groups) are often better prepared to cope with the ambiguities of life in new lands than those totally integrated into their old societies. Cultural factors are critical, too. Moving to a society like one's own is far easier than going into an entirely foreign one. Knowing the language of a new society is the most significant feature in acculturation, but so too, of course, are the talent, skills, and other training that are useful in the new society.

So there are advantaged and disadvantaged refugees. Still, while cultural familiarity, language ability, and technical competence may be necessary factors for easing adjustments, even they are not sufficient. Many worldly, articulate, highly trained refugees have, by virtue of their apparent ability to function in a new society, misled observers into believing that they are well-adjusted to their fate. The fact is that there is often a considerable gap between public personalities and private thoughts; many cosmopolites ache as much for home as the emblematic Madonna and the displaced peasant.

Dependency is a complex phenomenon in its own right, but so too is the idea of the obligation to assist and indeed the source of such obligation. As Dean Kitagawa noted, the sacred texts of many cultures indicate how one must deal with a stranger at the gate. In the Jewish tradition there is the admonition to love the stranger, "for we were strangers in the land of Egypt." It is a theme that reappears in the New Testament and is often expressed in parables such as that of the Good Samaritan. The Judeo/Christian tradition has counterparts in many others. For example, in Sophocles' *Oedipus at Colonus*, we are told how Theseus, king of Athens, welcomed the exiled Oedipus to his lands saying: "Never could I turn away from any stranger such as you are now and leave him to his fate."

In modern times, as in ancient ones, it can be a great help to the estranged when others extend the hand of welcome. It can be devastating to seekers of asylum when no humble samaritan or noble king stands by to assist. And yet the historic record shows that too often wariness has been more prevalent than acceptance, that far more barriers have been erected to prevent entry than bridges laid down to enhance it.

Fear of the stranger seems to be a more common sentiment than compassion. In his crude, simple, straightforward poetry, Rudyard Kipling had a most reasonable sociological explanation for this morally reprehensible tendency. You may remember the poem that begins:

> The stranger within my gate
> He may be true or kind,
> But he does not talk my talk.
> I cannot feel his mind.
> I see the face, the eyes, the mouth,
> But not the soul behind.
>
> The men of my own stock,
> They may do ill or well,
> But they tell the lies I'm wonted to.
> They are used to the lies I tell,
> And we don't need interpreters

When we go to buy and sell.

Kipling was writing of a phenomenon known in Theseus's day, and in our own, as xenophobia, the fear of the stranger. It is a far more widely held sentiment than its opposite, the love of the foreigner, which is often translated from the Greek of the New Testament as hospitality.

If xenophobia is so widespread a sentiment, how is it that any political sojourners have found refuge in others lands? The explanation lies in the broader social structural context. After all, refugees do not simply appear, they are products of upheaval within and between societies. Given this fact of social life, it is not at all surprising that many acts of assistance are offered not simply, solely, or even mainly because of biblical injunction or humanitarian concern, but for geopolitical reasons; often with diplomatic points being scored and debts paid, or heavy prices extracted for assisting the homeless, granting asylum.

While there is no question that there have always been generally charitable people who welcome the "weary pilgrims," protection and especially admission have often been provided on a highly selective basis. Only certain types of people have been permitted to come ashore, to cross the frontier, to enter closed communities.

In this century the control of borders has become a major social policy issue in many countries of the world. Restrictions motivated by political concerns have greatly complicated already serious social problems in many nations, including our own.

We need to remind ourselves that this nation, which began, with the words of that stirring Thanksgiving cantata, "When a band of exiles moored their boat on the wild New England shore," has not always treated seekers of sanctuary with equanimity. For many years there were laws on our books that blatantly discriminated against the entry of certain categories of would-be petitioners, and there were many exclusionary attitudes that denied asylum to many who, as Elie Wiesel reminded us, might have been saved from the Holocaust not so long ago.

Today many of the old restrictions have been lifted, and many of the explicit biases have been modified. Many who work with refugees point to the Refugee Act of 1980 as a major step forward in providing the framework to deal with those who suffered that categorical persecution we heard referred to before or who have a well-founded fear of persecution should they return or be returned to their homelands. However, as we have also heard, the Act did not provide refugee status for those who were in that twilight zone whom some call economic migrants, and all the groups in between.

In a recent paper appropriately called *The Conundrum of American Immigration and Refugee Policy*, political scientist Norman Zucker addressed himself to some of the paradoxes and pitfalls in some of our own recent policies, which he said are at times too rigid and too flexible. They are rigid, he noted, when authorities wish to stick to the letter of the law, as in the case of the controversies surrounding the INSing of young Khmer. They are flexible when it is politically expedient to bend the rules, as in permitting dubious applicants from Poland to be accepted as political refugees rather than as economic migrants.

While allotments for refugee admissions have been considerably more generous in recent years, U.S. actions in these realms are still essentially, I believe, reactions to particular political situations. The undercurrent of East/West politics remains a prominent factor enhancing the opportunities of some while inhibiting the access of others.

But it is not the only one. Special interest groups have long played a part in American political scenes. Bloc power, not Black power, is an old issue and it must also be reckoned with. Generally we think of it in terms of domestic affairs—pressures to advance civil rights, to legalize abortion, to get prayers back in school, to provide bilingual education. But, of course, pressures have long been exercised by powerful constituencies at home to affect immigration and refugee policy. We need think only of how and why amendment after amendment was tacked onto the Simpson/Mazzoli Bill in the last session of Congress. Some of those who have recently sought admission to the United States have benefited because they have very strong and very effective lobbyists championing their cause. That the cases of those such as Soviet Jews are just does not gainsay the fact that far fewer voices are raised to assist Haitians or Salvadorans or South Africans to get out of their repressive societies, or to ease their entry into this one.

Let me simply conclude by saying that there are two tendencies warring, as DuBois might have said, within one body of politics. There is a humanitarian proclivity, a genuine desire to play the role of the Good Samaritan, and it is deeply and genuinely felt by many who set, coordinate, and carry out American policies. But there is also the pressure of politics, the need to weigh difficult choices, to make tragic choices. When the two converge, as in the case of saving Vietnam's boat people, policy makers and implementers can be at once pure of heart and practically and politically pragmatic. But when moral sensibilities clash with national, ethnic, or local interests, it is time to call a conference like this.

# Updating the Golden Rule
## for the Global Village

## Roger Conner

It is difficult to face the necessity of limiting immigration. As someone who is married to the daughter of refugees from Lithuania and who has joyfully taken into our family a sister-in-law who is a refugee from Cuba, it is especially painful for me to confront the fact that we cannot take all of the world's dispossessed into the United States. But "truth, like roses, often comes with thorns," said the poet.

Why must we limit refugees? I suggest three fundamental reasons: the United States has changed; the world has changed; and immigration levels have changed. Let us look first at the *United States*. At the opening of this century, we imagined that we were a country of unlimited resources. Maybe with 90 or 100 million people, in effect, we were. Today, we recognize that our natural resources are finite and that the capacity of technology to stretch resources is not without limit.

The biologists and ecologists have introduced us all to the concept of carrying capacity. The idea is that our land, like any other ecosystem, has a carrying capacity. If we exceed it with numbers of people or technology that it cannot support, we will consign future generations to a permanently lowered quality of life. No one knows precisely what level of population we can support; part of the answer depends on how important wilderness, resource independence, or green space is to you. But many biologists argue that we are already near—or even beyond—the number we can permanently sustain in a quality lifestyle today, and they want to stabilize United States population growth now.

The second change in the United States is perhaps even more important. At the opening of this century we imagined this as a country of unlimited opportunity. Anyone who tried could become at least middle class, if not rich. We were different than the "old country," because in Europe there was an inherited lower class.

In the 1970s and 1980s, there is a growing body of evidence that class lines are hardening in this country. The social class, or the standard of living, of a child born today, is a better predictor of the way he will die than any other single factor. Indeed, since 1973 there has been no rise in the real standard of living of most Americans and there has been a decline in the real standard of living of about the bottom third of our entire society. The gap between the middle- and the lower-income groups in this country is growing. It is a new reality that we are no longer the land of unlimited opportunities.

Migration is not the sole cause of our inability to stabilize population growth and expand opportunities for disadvantaged American workers. But we can never achieve these goals without sharply limited migration.

The *world* has also changed since the opening of the century, in ways that are hard for us to grasp. The rate of annual population growth in the world for the last million years is two one-thousandths of one percent (.002 of 1%). The rate of population growth in the world for the last 20 years has been between one-and-one-half and two percent (1½% to 2%). It is hard for us to grasp the incredible magnitude of world population growth, but understanding these numbers is critical.

If an individual came to your door one night and said, "I am down on my luck. It is cold outside. I haven't any clothes. I haven't any food. If you could just give me a meal and a place to stay for the night, I will be on my way tomorrow," most of you would want to take that person in. If a family appeared on your doorstep and made the same request, you would call the county welfare office for assistance for the family. And if a village showed up on your doorstep, you would probably call the police. Numbers make a difference, and the numbers in the world have changed.

The second thing in the world that has changed, and Michael Teitelbaum referred to this a moment ago, is communication. We have all been told to "love thy neighbor as thyself," but we have not been told how I love my neighbor as myself and act on that when television has made every poor human being in the world my neighbor.

Let me ask you a question: How do you think the American people feel when they are told one more time, "You are not doing enough," "You are not admitting enough people," "You are wrong to feel that these people should be excluded"? Do they feel wicked because they are not doing more? They are beginning to feel that this is now more a case of the self-righteous browbeating the righteous.

A philosopher observed a century ago that if everyone is my brother, I have no brothers. The modern communications revolution has made us terribly aware of the plight of others, but at some point it begins to weaken the humanitarian response to the plight of each of the people that we see. So the world has changed, and in ways that make limits a necessity.

There is a third reason why refugee admissions have to be limited: *immigration* from other sources is high. Americans marry foreign nationals and want to bring them here. Americans who have immigrated to the United States want to bring their brothers and sisters and families here. American companies want to bring skilled workers here. Americans want to have maids at prices at which Americans are not willing to be maids. Employers want to bring in unskilled foreign workers, and if the laws won't allow them to be brought in legally, the American employers who want cheap labor are perfectly prepared to bring them in illegally. The result is that we are nearing record levels of total immigration.

Now, refugees are and should be a specially privileged type of immigrant. But refugees are immigrants. When you have 91% of the American people saying they want an all-out campaign to stop illegal immigration, and 80% repeatedly say that they would prefer total immigration of less than 400,000 a year, something must be done. The very existence of high levels of immigration from other sources makes limitation on refugee admissions a political reality.

Another factor I would call your attention to is that an incautious refugee policy may actually increase the number of people who decide to put themselves in the circumstance of seeking refugee status. If there is a perception abroad that the United States is prepared to take any refugee, there are world leaders who are prepared to manipulate that fact by expelling their people; Cuba and Vietnam are examples of this.

In addition, the standard of living in the United States is much higher than the standard of living in the Third World. If refugee resettlement is guaranteed here, it simply defies logic to suggest that people are not going to try to place themselves in refugee-like circumstances in order to qualify for immigration. For example, would there have been as many willing Cuban boat people if the destination had been Madrid or Caracas? I think not. Were the numbers increased once they knew we would accept them "with open arms"? The answer is obvious.

Given these reasons, there is almost a cry from the ordinary, grassroots American people that I encounter in my work as a member of a public interest group, a cry to you as the religious and moral leaders: How do we respond? How do we decide? How many? Who?

The response that you have given us so far about how to deal in the world of the 1980s is to recite to us the story of St. Martin of Tours. When he encountered the beggar on the road, he took half of his coat and gave it to the beggar. This is the story we are told, as if it were an answer. But the people that I have talked to say, "Wait a minute. That isn't enough. What if St. Martin had encountered twenty beggars? Would he have cut the coat into twenty little pieces, inadequate for each? Should he have chosen one? What would he have done?"

I think that new and more rigorous thinking on the philosophical and moral bases for deciding refugee admissions is urgently needed. Take a look at the marvelous book, *The Wall* by John Hersey. The protagonist is a Jew in the Warsaw ghetto. As the vise closes in he begins in a series of almost trance-like states to ask himself the questions: Whom do I die for? Whom do I give up food for, threatening my own life? Whom will I betray an associate for? As he begins to ask himself these questions, he comes up with a theory of concentric circles: the closer the relationship, the higher the obligations.

I offer this as only one example of the kind of rigorous, difficult thinking we need. Somehow we have to get beyond the stage where we are now. Although we realize that we can't take everybody, most of the groups represented here are willing to discuss only how to take more. We must get beyond that. Otherwise the decisions about the number of refugees are going to be left strictly to the political arena and to the most powerful pressure groups. The result will be a sort of "tyranny of adhocracy" rather than any sort of carefully reasoned choice.

# *Closing Remarks*

## John R. Silber

Dr. Teitelbaum has delineated tragic choices posed for us by the refugee problem. Defining the term "refugee" is, as Bishop Bevilacqua pointed out, less important than helping refugees. But it must be understood, as all members of Panel I made clear, that tragic choices are responses to tragic facts and that the latter remain, no matter what choices we make.

The practical consequence is that we cannot meet all the needs posed by refugees and hence we must choose among those millions who seek refuge in the United States: we must decide about policies—foreign, military, and domestic policies—that will affect the number of refugees in the world and the means of responding to their needs. Mr. Conner pointed out that our resources are limited and that the acceptance of refugees adversely affects—indeed punishes most severely—those Americans at the lowest levels of our economic and social orders.

I would observe that in matters of refugee policy, as in matters of public school administration, "solutions" are frequently urged that impose great suffering on one group in an effort to alleviate the suffering of others and that often these solutions are urged with enormous insensitivity by individuals who will not be affected one way or another by the imposition of the so-called solution. In this regard, and without the slightest forfeit of moral idealism, we would do well to recall the hard wisdom of W. B. Yeats: that reforms and revolutions and even good deeds do not necessarily produce improvements of any sort. Yeats wrote in "The Great Day":

> Hurrah for Revolution and more cannon shot!
> A beggar upon horseback lashes a beggar on foot.
> Hurrah for the Revolution and cannon come again!

The beggars have changed places, but the lash goes on.

Concern for all individual suffering and tragedy is an essential part of the sensibility of any decent person. But this infinite concern is an ineffectual and even dangerous and immoral basis on which to build public policy. We cannot develop a sound or just public policy on the basis of doing something that vastly transcends the capacity not only of individuals but of our nation itself.

If we are to have a just and effective national policy on refugees, we must address the issues in terms of our abilities and limitations.

It is the duty of a public official to seek a solution consistent with national survival, a solution protective of our own citizens. It is not fair to our minorities and our poor to undermine their positions and make "refugees" out of them in a maladroit effort to help refugees from other nations. When we admit refugees, we must share fairly at all socioeconomic levels the burden of their assimilation.

We must reject the cosmic guilt imposed on us by those who find us guilty of finitude and guilty of being confronted by tragic facts.

And we must certainly reject the ideologically-derived charge of guilt that imposes on the United States the blame for having created the refugee problem! To the extent that we are responsible for the refugee problem worldwide, it is because we have not linked our foreign and defense policies with an aim to reduce the number of refugees. If we had, we would have used our monopoly on nuclear arms (held from 1945 to 1952) to end *without bloodshed and without war* the Soviet occupation of Central Europe, which created millions of refugees. The production of refugees from Latvia, Lithuania, Estonia, Poland, East Germany, Czechoslovakia, Hungary, and Rumania continued until the Soviet Union completed the walls and fences across Central Europe and effectively entrapped and imprisoned those millions who were trying to get out! It was our failure to pursue the interests of the government of South Vietnam and to defeat the aggression from the North that resulted in the creation of millions of refugees from South Vietnam and later from Laos and

Cambodia. At this conference we should not allow ourselves to be led into an endorsement of the party line of the Soviet Union. If we had recognized the true situation in Vietnam and defeated the Northern invasion, we could have prevented the creation of Vietnamese, Cambodian, and Laotian refugees. To the extent that we are responsible, it is only for our failure to protect the freedom and liberty of the South Vietnamese. The direct responsibility, however, lies with the Soviet Union and its allies, which it supplied with military equipment—the North Vietnamese, the Pathet Lao, and the Khmer Rouge.

We must be neither crass nor complacent about refugee problems; neither must we contribute to indifference by beating our breasts over our "sin of finitude" nor accept the Soviet fiction that we are the threat to world peace and the enslavers of peoples. We did not invade Afghanistan. Nor did we invade El Salvador. The situation there is largely the consequence of the determined opposition by Marxists and by right wing oligarchs to the land reform efforts of a weak, centrist, freely elected government that—pressed from right and left—tries to uphold its democratic objectives. Its reform efforts and its dedication to democratic government have been frustrated by the intervention of forces supplied by Cuba and Soviet Union through Nicaragua.

We cannot solve the worldwide refugee problem without the maintenance of military forces that are greater than those most persons in this audience, I suspect, are prepared to support. It may be that there are those in this audience who share the objectives of the Grand Inquisitor, who prefer peace and material well-being to freedom.

Moreover, we cannot do anything significant to resolve the general problems of economic refugees without linking our programs of aid to programs of population control. The truth of the matter is this: *without the guidance of a hard head, there can be no truly compassionate heart.* Those of us who recognize the interconnection of economic, military, political, and linguistic issues in the resolution of refugee problems are neither negative nor pessimistic. We are, rather, thoughtfully optimistic, responsible idealists.

# *Closing Remarks*

## Peter I. Rose

I would like to add one thing. As others have reminded us, these are, at bottom, human problems. I think that the burden of those who cross the various seas of heartbreak can be eased by those of us here and those dedicated and skilled empathic workers with whom we work. I have seen them throughout Southeast Asia, Europe, and this country. But even they, or we, can only vicariously enter the minds and hearts of those who give up so much to find a safe haven and to start over.

As Bruce Grant said in *The Boat People*, "whether immigrants leave of their own initiative or as victims of historical events or of the harsh politics of discrimination, they are cutting ties with the land and the people of their birth; they are fleeing. It is one of the most fateful decisions a human being can make, or be forced to make. It means a break with all that one knows about living: how to earn a livelihood; how to respond to the landscape; how to touch and smell and taste." I just hope as we continue these deliberations, which surely will not end here, that those issues also will be in our minds.

# II. Response of the World Community to Refugees

Considering the pervasive character of the problems of refugees today, the tardy response of the world community to their plight is amazing. The first serious effort to deal with refugee problems was initiated in 1921 by the League of Nations, which appointed a High Commissioner for Russian and Armenian Refugees, respectively the victims of the Bolshevik Revolution and Turkish oppression. In 1933, the League again appointed a High Commissioner for Refugees to rescue Jewish and other victims of Nazi Germany, but the League received very little cooperation from its member nations. In the late 1930s an Intergovernmental Committee on Refugees (IGCR) was formed, but it, too, proved ineffective. More successful was the United Nations Relief and Rehabilitation Administration (UNRRA), which during the period between 1943 and 1947 managed to repatriate an impressive number of anti-Nazis and anti-Facist refugees. In 1947, the United Nations created the International Refugee Organization (IRO); but its mandate expired after five years, leaving 15,000,000 refugees unsettled. Meanwhile, the Intergovernmental Committee for European Migration (ICEM) was organized outside of the United Nations framework; initially representing sixteen, but finally more than thirty, concerned nations, this organization had an excellent record in resettling large numbers of European refugees, including 160,000 who fled Hungary after the 1956 revolution. Since 1950, the Office of the United Nations High Commissioner for Refugees (UNHCR) has been hard at work, with an inadequate budget, promoting and coordinating legal and political resolutions concerning the future of refugees, helping some to return voluntarily to their own homelands, assisting others to remain in the country of first asylum, or resettling them in other countries. The United Nations also created the United Nations Relief and Works Agency for Palestinian Refugees (UNRWA) in 1949 and the United Nations Korean Reconstruction Agency (UNKRA) in 1951.

As might be expected, the International Refugee Organization works closely with governments and agencies of concerned nations. It also depends heavily upon international religious and welfare organizations, for example, the World Council of Churches Refugee Service, the National Catholic Welfare Conference, the Hebrew Immigrant Aid Society, the International Social Service, the International Rescue Committee, the YMCA, and a number of religious and private agencies in various nations. Since 1962, the International Council of Volunteer Agencies (ICVA), which now has over one hundred member organizations, has been promoting both interagency cooperation and the participation of private citizens.

It is worth noting that the cause of refugees was greatly enhanced by the 1951 Convention Relating to the Status of Refugees and its updated 1967 Protocol. These bodies were instrumental in defining refugees as people who, "owing to well-founded fear of being persecuted for reasons of race, religion, nationality, membership of a particular social group, or political opinion, are outside their country of nationality and are unable, or owing to such fear, are unwilling to avail themselves of the protection of their country." It must be remembered, however, that there are many *de facto* refugees, for example, victims of a disastrous economy or of civil strife, who are not covered by the United Nations definition of refugees. It is highly significant that the signatory nations of the Convention and the Protocol accepted the principle of non-refoulement, which assures that refugees will not be sent back by force to countries where their life or liberty is at stake.

Equally important are the two recent expressions of the world community: (1) the Universal Declaration of Human Rights, which affirms the individual's right to seek and enjoy asylum; and (2) the Declaration of Territorial Asylum, which urges all nations to grant asylum to those who seek it. Although these two documents are not legally binding, signatory nations are morally obligated to abide by their principles. Yet the fact remains that it is the prerogative of each sovereign nation either to grant or to withhold asylum. Currently many Western nations, overwhelmed by the sudden increase of asylum seekers, seem to be trying to reduce the refugee flow; and in the economically less fortunate nations of the Third World, the steady increase of refugees adds a great burden to their already limited national resources.

The available channels appear inadequate to enable the world community to share in the burden of the refugee problem. How can we establish feasible international standards for sharing the cost and burdens of refugee care and resettlement? Is large-scale repatriation a workable option for refugees from Third World countries? If not, where should they be encouraged to resettle—in the Third World or Western nations, and on what grounds? What are, or ought to be, the motivations and moral responsibilities of more affluent nations vis à vis refugees and asylees?

# Introduction*

## Peter Gomes

It is my happy task to serve as the moderator for this second panel, which is concerned with the subject of the response of the world community to the question of refugees with which we have concerned ourselves this morning.

The temptation is always strong for the moderator to get his licks in first, and I am not above temptation.

The year 1820, as you may know, was the nation's first bicentennial—that is, the 200th anniversary of the landing of the Pilgrims at Plymouth Rock. That landing has provided, in a very real way, both the inspiration and part of the dilemma with which we, as a nation, have ever since been confronted as to the nature of our borders, the nature of our society, and our responsibility and obligations to the world.

By 1820 the Pilgrims had ceased to be simply immigrants and refugees and had, in fact, become the spiritual progenitors of the kingdom of heaven on earth. This metamorphosis from exiles and refugees to founding fathers, mothers, children and heirs, is one of the most remarkable bits of sociological alchemy. It suggests, as one of our speakers earlier noted, that anything is possible and everything is possible.

Let me read just a line or two of Daniel Webster's discourse delivered at Plymouth on December 22, 1820, in commemoration of the first settlement from England, to set the tone and describe the mood with which we continue to contend today:

Forever honored be this, the place of our fathers' refuge.

Forever remember the day which saw them weary and distressed, broken in everything but spirit, poor in all but faith and courage.

At last secure from the dangers of wintery seas, and impressing the shore with the first footsteps of civilized man.

How we deal with that inheritance, imagined in some respects and real in others, is the continuing agenda which confronts us today.

# Morality and Resettlement

## R. Richard Rubottom

I feel privileged to be a part of this distinguished panel to open the discussion on response of the world community to the ethical issues involved in the problem of refugees. The Department of State and the Religious Advisory Committee should be congratulated for having planned a program based on such a timely subject.

I sense a deep and gnawing concern on the part of the American people with respect to the overall situation pertaining to immigration, and the related subject of refugees. This is reflected in the amount of coverage given to these subjects in the press and in the electronic media. It is also seen in the degree of support given to the Federation for American Immigration Reform. Perhaps most importantly, these subjects are now being reviewed and discussed widely in church settings throughout the United States, as, for example, the all-day program sponsored by Church Women United held recently in Dallas.

This is good news, and not a moment too soon. The United States has reached a major threshold in its attempt to deal with the problems of immigration and refugees. The initiative rests with the Congress. Either it summons the will to pass a bill and send it to the President for signature, or our nation will continue to drift on this issue, only postponing the inevitable judgment day when the solution, whatever it is, will be more difficult than now.

I have been asked to address the question of whether large-scale repatriation is possible for a majority of refugees from Third World countries or whether third-country resettlement is a more realistic option. As one from the university community, I wish I could say that I had traveled to refugee settlements to make case studies among refugees themselves or that I had taken polls within carefully selected professional and citizen groups of certain indicated countries to obtain opinions that might throw light on this very difficult question. But I have not done either of those tasks.

However, drawing on my experience and reading, and on the opinion of the experts who wrote the study papers for the Aspen Institute Steering Committee on Western Hemisphere Governance on which I served for two and one-half years, I would say that in the short run third-country resettlement of refugees is the more realistic option, *as discouraging as that prospect might be.* The United States should, as it has been doing, play a leading role in providing the means and the method for handling this extraordinary burden of resettlement. I refer, of course, not only to our government but to the countless private organizations, especially church-related groups, which have demonstrated their humanitarian concern for the lives and well-being of the human beings involved. The task is enormous. No single nation, however well-motivated, can do it alone. But by sharing the burden, much can be accomplished, as the record shows.

Fortunately, the United Nations High Commissioner for Refugees (UNHCR) has a vast reservoir of experience and shares our concern in dealing with this problem, than which there is none more tragic in its human dimension. The role of those countries already providing refuge should be publicly recognized. In addition to statements of gratitude and appreciation, "they need and deserve the help of the concerned international community."[1]

Let us consider three questions with deeply moral, as well as political, dimensions. The first one: With problems of hunger, even survival, being given priority in two-thirds of the world's nation states, how can they summon the will and the means to express compassion for refugees from other nations, and then convert that feeling into a viable, affordable national policy? Somehow, some way, the presence of the refugees, especially in nations which have so far looked the other way, has to be converted into a plan for action of enlightened self-interest. In the divine plan for the human beings who populate this world, their moral worth weighs most heavily in the scales, but within each being there is intrinsic worth more valuable than any purely material resource. In the human capacity to love and care, to think and act, and to work and produce, we see our uniqueness. It is in the divine combination of these traits that human beings have transcended difficulties since the beginning of time, and, just as surely, they will transcend this difficulty. One can pray that in the latter part of this twentieth century the right equation of compassion and self-interest will be found.

The second question: If treating others the way one wishes to be treated, sometimes called the Golden Rule, is axiomatic in nearly all the world's major religions, as I understand it is, can those words be translated into deeds? Could they possibly apply to refugee policy around the world? Here the crying need is the exemplar role. Perhaps if one nation, then two or three nations, and then a dozen nations were to set the example, others might follow. To repeat, no one nation can do it alone. "Burden-sharing is central to a successful international approach to refugee assistance."[2]

The third question is a moral one. It is one I have asked my classes at the university, and many audiences like this one. Is it necessary that the world be engulfed in war for us, its citizens, to find the moral strength and commitment to defend great ethical principles? How much is human dignity and well-being worth to us? Do we of the developed nations think we can survive for long if our fellow beings in more than half the world have no hope to improve their state of bare subsistence? I don't know the answer, but I place my trust in the belief that we shall find an awesome response to an awesome challenge. The Marshall Plan was one such response. The regional banks, especially the Inter-American Bank, are another (and one we had rejected for fifty years before we saw the light).

Let me raise one final political consideration as evidence of a well-intentioned action which had adverse repercussions, repercussions which should have been foreseen. In 1963, the United States was anguishing over whether or not to abrogate unilaterally the Migrant Labor Agreement which had been in effect with Mexico since 1951, an action which finally took place the following year, 1964. During the course of the public discussion, the then Mexican ambassador, Lic. Antonio Carrillo Flores, made a prophetic statement:

It is not to be expected that the termination of an international agreement governing and regulating the rendering of service of Mexican workers in the U.S. will put an end to that type of seasonal migration. The agreement is not the cause of that migration; it is the effect or result of the migratory phenomena. Therefore, the absence of an agreement would not end the problem but rather would give rise to a de facto situation: the illegal introduction of Mexican workers into the U.S.

The ambassador was right. By its action, the United States transformed the Mexican migrant worker, who with legal status would complete his assignment and return home, into an undocumented alien, and ultimately a refugee, to be joined by millions of others like him; and they are still coming, since we apparently have neither the will nor the means to stop their entry.

We Americans are an enigma to our friends as well as our adversaries. On the one hand, we are pragmatic and tough-minded; on the other, we are compassionate and generous. Which of the many faces of America is the real one? Perhaps others can answer that better than I, but of one thing I feel reasonably sure—whatever generous motives our government has in response to citizens at large are largely hidden by the need to justify every government appropriation in terms of self-interest. We have become experts at intellectual and economic rationalization of American assistance programs while abjuring the moral rationalization which reflects the true feeling, I am confident, of the vast majority of our citizens.

The time is short. The need is great. I trust that if we do more, others will follow.

*Notes*

1. Statement of Acting Secretary Kenneth Dam, September 29, 1982, before the Senate Judiciary Committee.
2. Ibid.

# International Standards on Refugee Assistance

## Leo Cherne

Destiny can take many forms—biological, geographical, manifest. For refugees and for questions surrounding their care and resettlement, destiny in all its forms has special relevance.

I have been asked to discuss common international standards for the sharing of costs and burdens of refugee care and resettlement: do such standards exist? what are they? can they be improved? I am tempted to give simplistic answers to these questions as did the president of Citibank when asked how many people worked there: "About half," was his laconic reply.

First of all, there are no common international standards for sharing the costs nor should there be, unless one were willing to settle for the lowest common denominator in international conduct; and destiny—biological, geographical, and manifest—precludes such a settlement.

In refugee matters, destiny as *biology* is revealed in the common ties of ethnicity and shared ancestry that bind particular groups of persons to one another. For example, it is not simply by political fiat that nearly three million refugees from Afghanistan have been welcomed into Pakistan. The majority of these refugees are "cousins" to the Pathans of the northwest frontier province, and share with them both blood ties and deep cultural, religious, and spiritual values and traditions. The postwar movements of Jews to Israel and other lands which continue today, the flow of Germans from East to West before the building of the Wall, and the pervasive sense of oneness in Chinese culture that all but eclipses political or ideological differences within their societies are all indicative of a biological or ethnic destiny whose strength cannot be measured and which asserts itself time and time again in the affairs of mankind in ways often more irrational than rational, more illogical than logical, and which defies international norms or standards for the sharing of burdens.

The destiny imposed upon refugees by *geography* is every bit as compelling as the destiny of biology. When people were forced to flee from Ethiopia, neighboring Sudan or Somalia were their inevitable destinations. Cambodians and Laotians seeking to escape from the Communist oppressors have only one place to go: Thailand. For Cubans, the United States is the logical place of refuge, as Scandinavia would be for Poles if they were forced to flee from their homeland.

Sovereign states rarely seek to become havens of first asylum for their neighbors in distress. But history—or is it destiny?—often propels such states into this role. History also shows that those countries that have been so challenged and propelled have usually benefited from accepting their destiny with grace. With few exceptions—and the Middle East is the most notorious—nations which have accepted the responsibility of becoming a country of first asylum have not only won respect but also have enhanced their own security and have attracted large amounts of financial and material aid from the international community. One can argue persuasively that by recognizing their geographical destiny, Thailand, Pakistan, the Sudan, and Somalia have done well by doing good. Austria, despite its proximity to the Soviet Union and the Warsaw Pact forces, has consistently provided sanctuary for those fleeing the U.S.S.R. and its East European satellites; and by recognizing the destiny of its geography, Austria has turned a liability into an asset, winning the respect of all, benefiting materially, and enhancing its security. These nations have not acted because of any accepted international standards of burden-sharing. Circumstances dictated pragmatic responses based on estimates of the vital national interests of the particular society rather than on some international table of values.

The *manifest destiny* of refugees results primarily from the actions of man rather than from accidents of biology or geography. Nations, individually or in groups, assume special relationships with other nations, singly or collectively, based on the intersections of their destinies. These relationships imply certain privileges and advantages as well as certain responsibilities and obligations. The privileges and advantages of colonialism waned and were replaced by responsibilities and obligations as the winds of independence blew across the developing world. Particular responsibilities have devolved on all former colonial powers, but especially on the United Kingdom, France, Portugal, Belgium, and the Netherlands. Added to the postcolonial experience are the continued and protracted tensions engendered by the Cold War, which has produced the Iron Curtain, the Bamboo Curtain, and overseas adventures that have created untold millions of uprooted persons and homeless refugees. Decisions made in Moscow, Peking, and Washington have the gravest and most immediate consequences on the peoples in Saigon, Kabul, and Addis Ababa, thousands of miles away. It is not surprising that the Communist takeover in Indochina has resulted in massive refugee flows, or that the Soviet intervention in Afghanistan has driven people out, or that Cuban mercenaries operating in Africa have sent people running.

One can chastise these refugee-creating societies for their sins of both commission and omission, for ironically they almost invariably refuse to share in the burdens they create. But chastisement neither relieves the refugees' problems nor absolves societies that value human life and individual dignity from the moral obligation to aid the oppressed. But here again international standards are meaningless, except as guides and examples for others—and here the standards should be the highest attainable.

There are three basic ways to measure international performances in response to refugee emergencies: (1) the amount of money contributed to refugee assistance on a per capita basis; (2) the number of refugees accepted for resettlement in relation to the host country's population; (3) the number of refugees in first asylum in a given country in relation to the host country's population.

(1) the 1983 pledges to the United Nations High Commissioner for Refugees (Table 1) indicates the following countries lead in per capita dollar contributions to refugee assistance.

| | | |
|---|---|---|
| Norway | $1.52 | per person |
| Sweden | .98 | " |
| Denmark | .70 | " |
| Australia | .51 | " |
| U.S.A. | .34 | " |
| Switzerland | .31 | " |
| Japan | .25 | " |
| Canada | .16 | " |

(2) The most accessible current resettlement figures pertain to the Indochinese refugees, of whom some 1,250,000 have found new homes since 1975 (Table 2). On a per capita basis, i.e., the number of refugees resettled divided by the total population, the leading countries appear to be:

| Australia | .005% of the population |
|-----------|-------------------------|
| Canada | .004% " |
| U.S.A. | .003% " |
| France | .002% " |

(3) Of the countries of first asylum, the overwhelming burden—or highest standard—falls on three countries which rank among the neediest in terms of their own economic development: Somalia, the Sudan, and Pakistan. The ratios of refugees in first asylum to overall population are:

| Somalia | 25% of the population |
|---------|-----------------------|
| Sudan | 5% " |
| Pakistan | 4% " |

Yet regardless of formula the realities reassert themselves: there are simply no standards by which responses to refugee emergencies can be measured. Each situation has its own dynamics. Each country has its own vested interests, traditions, and political history. Each society has its own standards of conduct, ethical values, and moral codes. What is constant is the need for leadership, for the setting of examples, for courageous actions—these to be undertaken willingly, without invidious comparisons. Above and beyond the destinies of biology, geography, and manifest action is the collective destiny of the human race. If we pause to devise acceptable standards, or to carp at others who we feel may be lagging, we do so at our own peril.

# TABLE 1

## 1983 Contributions to UNHCR Assistance Activities
## (in U.S. Dollars)
## Situation as of February 16, 1983

| DONOR | GENERAL PROGRAMS | SPECIAL PROGRAMS | TOTAL PROGRAMS |
|---|---|---|---|
| **GOVERNMENTS** | | | |
| Algeria . . . . . . . . . . . . | 50,000 | | 50,000 |
| Australia . . . . . . . . . . . | 7,673,077 | | 7,673,077 |
| Austria . . . . . . . . . . . . | 100,000 | | 100,000 |
| Belgium . . . . . . . . . . . | 468,085 | | 468,085 |
| Benin . . . . . . . . . . . . . | 2,000 | | 2,000 |
| Brazil . . . . . . . . . . . . . | 15,000 | | 15,000 |
| Canada . . . . . . . . . . . . | 4,065,041 | | 4,065,041 |
| Chile . . . . . . . . . . . . . | 20,000 | | 20,000 |
| China . . . . . . . . . . . . . | 300,000 | | 300,000 |
| Colombia . . . . . . . . . . | 18,000 | | 18,000 |
| Cyprus . . . . . . . . . . . . | 3,659 | | 3,659 |
| Denmark . . . . . . . . . . . | 2,380,952 | 1,190,476 | 3,571,428 |
| Djibouti . . . . . . . . . . . | 2,000 | | 2,000 |
| Finland . . . . . . . . . . . . | 660,377 | | 660,377 |
| France . . . . . . . . . . . . . | 1,094,891 | | 1,094,891 |
| Germany (Federal Republic of) . . . . . . . | | 883,742 | 883,742 |
| Greece . . . . . . . . . . . . | 90,000 | | 90,000 |
| Holy See . . . . . . . . . . . | 2,500 | | 2,500 |
| Israel . . . . . . . . . . . . . | 20,000 | | 20,000 |
| Italy . . . . . . . . . . . . . | 341,297 | | 341,297 |
| Japan . . . . . . . . . . . . . | 3,000,000 | | 3,000,000 |

| DONOR | GENERAL PROGRAMS | SPECIAL PROGRAMS | TOTAL PROGRAMS |
|---|---|---|---|
| **GOVERNMENTS** | | | |
| Kuwait . . . . . . . . . . . . | 40,000 | | 40,000 |
| Lao People's Democratic Republic . . . . . | 6,000 | | 6,000 |
| Lebanon . . . . . . . . . . . . | 10,000 | | 10,000 |
| Luxembourg . . . . . . . . | 6,915 | | 6,915 |
| Malawi . . . . . . . . . . . . | 270 | | 270 |
| Malaysia . . . . . . . . . . . | 20,000 | | 20,000 |
| Mexico . . . . . . . . . . . . | 40,000 | | 40,000 |
| Monaco . . . . . . . . . . . . | 1,168 | | 1,168 |
| Morocco . . . . . . . . . . . | 10,000 | | 10,000 |
| Nigeria . . . . . . . . . . . . | 100,000 | | 100,000 |
| Norway . . . . . . . . . . . . | 5,213,280 | 1,142,857 | 6,356,137 |
| Oman . . . . . . . . . . . . . | 6,000 | | 6,000 |
| Pakistan . . . . . . . . . . . | 3,876 | | 3,876 |
| Panama . . . . . . . . . . . . | 500 | | 500 |
| Philippines . . . . . . . . . . | 6,000 | | 6,000 |
| Portugal . . . . . . . . . . . | 100,000 | | 100,000 |
| Qatar . . . . . . . . . . . . . | 35,000 | | 35,000 |
| Republic of Korea . . . . | 10,000 | | 10,000 |
| Saudi Arabia . . . . . . . . | 10,000 | | 10,000 |
| Senegal . . . . . . . . . . . . | 3,000 | | 3,000 |
| Spain . . . . . . . . . . . . . | 80,000 | | 80,000 |
| Sudan . . . . . . . . . . . . . | 2,308 | | 2,308 |
| Swaziland . . . . . . . . . . | 1,330 | | 1,330 |
| Sweden . . . . . . . . . . . . | 5,753,425 | 2,465,753 | 8,219,178 |
| Switzerland . . . . . . . . . | 2,010,050 | | 2,010,050 |
| Syrian Arab Republic . | 1,000 | | 1,000 |
| Thailand . . . . . . . . . . . | 10,000 | | 10,000 |

| DONOR | GENERAL PROGRAMS | SPECIAL PROGRAMS | TOTAL PROGRAMS |
|---|---|---|---|
| **GOVERNMENTS** | | | |
| Tunisia . . . . . . . . . . . . | 4,918 | | 4,918 |
| Turkey . . . . . . . . . . . . . | 11,000 | | 11,000 |
| United Kingdom . . . . . | | 48,387 | 48,387 |
| United Republic of Cameroon . . . . . . | 5,831 | | 5,831 |
| United States of America . . . . . . . | 78,000,000 | | 78,000,000 |
| Viet Nam . . . . . . . . . . | 1,000 | | 1,000 |
| Yugoslavia . . . . . . . . . | 30,000 | | 30,000 |
| Zimbabwe . . . . . . . . . . | 27,115 | | 27,115 |
| | 111,866,865 | 5,731,215 | 117,598,090 |
| **NON-GOVERNMENTAL ORGANIZATIONS AND OTHERS** . . . . . . | 645,876 | 288,722 | 934,598 |
| GRAND TOTAL | 112,512,741 | 6,019,937 | 118,532,678 |

# *TABLE 2*

## *Indochinese Refugees*
## *Countries of Resettlement*

| COUNTRY | INDO-CHINESE REFUGEES | POPULATION | REFUGEES PER CAPITA |
|---------|-----------------------|------------|---------------------|
| Australia | 75,000 | 15,000,000 | .005 |
| Canada | 90,000 | 24,000,000 | .004 |
| France | 100,000 | 54,000,000 | .002 |
| U.S.A. | 635,000 | 226,000,000 | .003 |

# Principles of Obligation and Burden-Sharing

## Silvano M. Tomasi

I. Are Western nations responding to refugee problems today more out of a sense of guilt than a sense of mission?

As formulated, the question is ambivalent. Guilt and mission are words used by theologians more than policy-makers, and I doubt that the ethical implications of guilt or mission are very decisive in determining government action. Self-interest is a more likely reason for political decisions. England or France probably do not feel too guilty about the fact that the boundaries of their former colonies in Africa cut across the territory of ethnic groups and that this legacy adds to the generation of refugees.

Until 1980 the U.S. legal definition of a refugee was set in the context of the relations between the West and the Soviet Union and their competitive economic and political systems. In this framework the actual resettlement of refugees in this country has been logically patterned as evidence of the failures of leftist regimes. This is the case of post-World War II refugees from Eastern Europe, Hungary, Cuba, and Vietnam.

On the other hand, the Refugee Act of 1980 restated a deeply rooted national conviction:

> The Congress declares that it is the *historic policy* of the United States to respond to the urgent needs of persons subject to persecution in their homelands, including, where appropriate, humanitarian assistance for their care and maintenance in asylum areas, efforts to promote opportunities for resettlement or voluntary repatriation, aid for necessary transportation and processing, admission to this country of refugees of special humanitarian concern

to the United States, and transitional assistance to refugees in the United States. . . . (Sec. 101(a)).

In more expressive language, accepting the Republican nomination (July 1980) for president, Ronald Reagan reformulated the oldest theme of American heritage:

Can we doubt that only a Divine Providence placed this land, *this island of freedom, here as a refuge* for all those people in the world who yearn to breathe freely: Jews and Christians enduring persecutions beyond the Iron Curtain, the boat people of Southeast Asia, of Cuba and of Haiti, the victims of drought and famine in Africa, the Freedom Fighters of Afghanistan, and our own countrymen held in savage captivity.

Political expediency, however, twists high principles into contradictory policies and inconsistent treatment. Thus extended voluntary departure is allowed for Ethiopians and Poles (two unfriendly governments) but not for Salvadorans and Guatemalans (two friendly governments). Should there be such a distinction if government acts out of a sense of mission?

Hospitality and hostility to immigrants and refugees are an existential dimension, contradictory and real, of American history. Political reality suggests that such ambivalence, if anything, will become more acute.

The maintenance of living standards, community expectations, and social values will tend to impose limits on any humanitarian response, especially if high unemployment and slow economic growth persist. Thus in West Germany until 1980, asylum-seekers could disembark and apply for asylum. It could take up to eight years of litigation before a final decision was rendered, and in the meantime applicants could enjoy all forms of assistance. The litigation process has been cut down to three years, and many of the economic rights, previously automatic, have been rescinded. Some applicants for asylum (e.g., Pakistanis and Bengali) are not allowed to disembark.

The increasing numbers of actual and potential refugees, lack of empty spaces, and economic crises are creating a restrictionist mood. Perhaps national policies will move further away from the traditional concept of acceptance of a substantial number of refugees to more immediate concerns with domestic needs as criteria for annual quotas of refugee intake.

While the ideal humanitarian response would be based primarily on the urgency of the condition of refugees as persons threatened in their basic rights and, therefore, with a claim on our solidarity, a breakdown of a sense of moral responsibility tends to insulate Western nations in the defense of their immediate well-being, only to obscure any sense of "mission."

Confronted with the influx of refugees in developing countries, the Western countries seem to devise new types of response that attempt to balance humanitarian concerns and national priorities and to keep a sense of moral commitment:

1. The frame of reference for the discussion and the long-range solution of refugee movements has changed from the East-West political and ideological competition to the North-South relationship in terms of development.

2. Switching the focus of attention from the right to emigrate and to a safe haven to the right to remain in one's country has led some observers to propose political mechanisms which will consider the means of averting mass flows and of assessing the relationship between mass exodus and the full enjoyment of human rights.

3. The international community is asked to exercise its sense of solidarity through a sharing of refugee problems fair to the refugees and to the country receiving the influx.

Developed countries are not just proposing alternatives that are of difficult practical implementation, but have also taken some steps that make more credible their solidarity with the Third World. In a few years the budget of the United Nations High Commission on Refugees (UNHCR) has passed from 7 to 500 million dollars, several thousand refugees have been successfully resettled in the West, and a concerted effort has been undertaken on the part of experts and scholars to refine the legal concepts and international instruments dealing with the protection of refugees.

A limited goal that would strengthen the disaster relief or social welfare work of the world community would be more effective supranational administration of relief resources. On a national level, efforts are always made to depoliticize welfare for unemployed, handicapped, and other persons with claim to community solidarity. A question could be raised if on the international level, in a parallel way, humanitarian assistance to refugees would not be more objective and effective if made more independent of national foreign policy interests.

If more power were given to the UNHCR or other United Nations or international structures so as to allow intervention to prevent refugee generation or to act immediately in a crisis, it would be easier to deduce that rich countries are acting out of a sense of mission. The same reasoning would hold if the United States, for example, were to adopt the definition of refugee contained in the 1969 Organization of African Unity Convention on Refugees, a less restrictive definition than that of 1951, and much more suitable to solve some current problems with refugees from Latin America.

I am afraid that it is easier to raise questions than to provide answers. Could the giving of more money to the UNHCR (e.g., the case of Japan) be a conscience relief for not taking in refugees? Or, if more power were given to the UNHCR so that in consultation with governments it could allocate quotas of refugees to be resettled in Western nations, would these nations accept?

In the context of guilt, it could be argued that it had an effect in the acceptance of Indochinese refugees in large numbers. If there were a strong perception that a country had a hand in creating a refugee situation, this country would probably be under strong moral pressure to take as many refugees as possible. How could a government be made to accept responsibility in a situation or country that is generating refugees? Could guilt have a triggering effect for solidarity?

II. How does the guilt/mission attitude affect the amount and character of assistance Western nations are willing to give to refugees?

The track record of financial assistance and resettlement of Western countries has been improving in recent years. The European Economic Community (EEC), the U.S.A., Japan, and other nations have increased the amount of their financial contributions of the UNHCR and to other programs for refugees.

In 1979 eighty-six countries out of 153 U.N. members contributed to the assistance of refugees, but only a handful gave substantially. Self-interest reasons will probably continue to determine how much financial aid can be given, how many refugees can be accepted for resettlement, how long a temporary refuge can be guaranteed to a group of refugees, or how many refugees can be integrated into development projects of a country of first asylum.

The ambivalence toward hospitality and national comfort is not just a dimension of American history. The conflict is the same everywhere, between a view of global coresponsibility, based on the transcultural and transnational foundation of the dignity of each person, and national exclusivism. If the first prevails, then the search for adequate response to refugee crises will remain a dynamic force that will produce new and better results.

In the process of meeting the recent refugee migrations, there has been also a sharpening of intervention strategies:

1. First of all, the conviction seems to have become stronger that refugee problems should be faced in a systematic and well-planned way at the levels of knowledge and policy, as an unwanted, but predictable, factor.

2. The immediate availability of resources when a crisis explodes is now seen as a necessity, and the first moves have been made, or are proposed, for a solution through funds like the Fund for Durable Solutions of the UNHCR and the Common Fund under the Integrated Program for Commodities of the U.N. Conference on Trade and Development.

3. Universal participation (as I mentioned before) in the welfare of refugees is finding application in the strengthening of the UNHCR machinery; in possible regional bureaus for "burden-sharing," like the Bureau for the Placement and Education of African Refugees (BPEAR), even though it has had limited successes; in the proposed allocation of quotas of refugees to industrialized countries on the basis of their

population and gross national product; in U.N. convening of special meetings of countries for specific crises; etc.

In conclusion, perhaps there should be a sense of guilt and a positive attitude of mission in the Western countries. It is not by chance, in fact, that the economic order and present geopolitics are what they are. There would be a greater incentive to understand the enormous complexity of today's refugee problems in the only context where a durable solution will be found: human solidarity.

# Closing Remarks

## R. Richard Rubottom

Our moderator for the second panel, Dr. Peter Gomes, took us back about 162 years to the 200th anniversary of the landing of the Mayflower. He read us a statement by Daniel Webster which reminded us of our beginnings as a nation. Leo Cherne cautioned against softening the tragic choices we may face by blurring or distorting our approaches. He urged especially that the distinction between refugees and economic migrants not be used to reduce urgent and legitimate needs. Cherne also emphasized that amongst foreigners joining us in the United States, refugees were an insignificant number: only 90,000 compared with 500,000 immigrants, one million or more visitors who don't leave, and some 500,000 annual illegal immigrants, whose number is rising. Finally, he counseled that the self-image we have of ourselves, and the view that the world has of our welcoming heritage, will entail cost as long as that is the way we wish to see ourselves and to be seen by others.

Father Tomasi said that Western nations tend to respond to refugee problems with an ambivalent attitude. From a Judeo-Christian ethical stand, there is a sense of responsibility to the entire human family. However, because of domestic needs and foreign policy constraints, high principles become twisted in the formulation of policies, with national or individual needs becoming so dominant as to obscure the larger picture. He continued by saying that recent mass refugee influxes are stirring up, through the media, a new awareness, and the ambivalence becomes more acute. Thus new steps are being proposed to safeguard a sense of moral responsibility. Examples of these recent developments are proposals for separating aid for refugees from foreign policy concerns, sharing with all countries the responsibility for resettlement and provision of resources, resettlement in the context of development projects, enlarging the definition of refugees, facing refugee problems not as ad hoc crises but as part of the global condition, and placing emphasis on human rights in the country producing refugees. As Father Tomasi concluded, the enormously complex issues of refugee immigration can be faced productively by choosing the only available option consistent with American history, namely, human solidarity.

I want to take a moment here for my part to stress something that has not been stressed enough today, and which, had I not been so constrained by time, I would have included in my remarks. I believe there is a responsibility that evolves upon all of our institutions and upon us as individuals to recognize the problem of getting back to the source of the difficulty within the countries that produced the refugees: the political, economic, and social problems. Without intervening directly in the affairs of these countries that are producing the refugees, we can do a great deal, and we must try to do more, to deal with the problem at the place where it originates. I think this is something that needs to be emphasized a great deal more.

I wish that Senator Simpson were still here, because I have become very interested in the immigration problem over the years. I have had some differences with the draft of the bill which passed the Senate last year, but I assume that everybody is hoping that it behooves all of us, as people who are interested in this subject and as concerned laymen and churchmen, to think about the political process and whether it has been designed to achieve the maximum practical result for the good of our nation.

Finally, I feel that, in spite of the fact that we are all human and need to be reinforced, the thrust of this meeting has been directed at the already converted. Somehow I would like to see the kind of discussion that we have had today, and the kind of thoughtful remarks that have been placed upon our minds and conscience, taken out into the American community at large. I have the feeling that without spending a lot of money, by drawing upon the talents that are here and the talents that are in our institutions and organizations scattered across the country, we could do a great deal in the way of education, information, and communication to an interested public. We have heard

Senator Simpson describe how much ignorance there is abroad; and I mean abroad within our own boundaries. So we haven't done the job if we stop here. I urge us to get this message out and to get the listening that we need to get from our people. And maybe we could learn from that process as well.

# III. United States Refugee Policy and Ethical Principles

Historically the United States has presented itself as a haven for the "huddled masses yearning to breathe free" from the teeming shores of other lands, and imposed virtually no restrictions for immigration until 1875. Since then, the American approach to immigration has vacillated between humanitarian and egalitarian ideals on the one hand and more elitist and restrictive measures on the other. This vacillation accounts for years of heated controversies over immigration policies between advocates of admissions leniency and advocates of admissions control. The quota system, which was introduced in 1921 to restrict immigration in favor of certain nationality groups, and which was revised and amended several times, was finally abolished in 1968.

The international situation following World War II created an ever growing number of displaced persons on various continents. In 1947, 1950, and 1953 the Congress of the United States enacted temporary laws to permit the entry of over 400,000 refugees and displaced persons, and in 1980 it passed the first Refugee Act in order to codify laws regarding refugees. Ironically, in the days after the passage of the Refugee Act some 125,000 Cuban refugees arrived and were processed by special legislation apart from the newly established Act. The events in Southeast Asia and Central America have also continued to produce more refugees who seek entry into the United States, Thus the United States has now suddenly become the country of "first asylum," a situation which has far-reaching implications. Caught by such a sudden influx of refugees from Haiti and El Salvador in addition to those from Cuba, the United States has resorted to various measures, including interdiction, detention, rejection, and even forced repatriation—measures which have touched off a series of protests from humanitarian and religious groups. Yet many people are deeply concerned by the fact that the backlog of asylum petitions to the United States has already exceeded 100,000 in number and probably will not decrease in the forseeable future. In addition, it appears that the problem of illegal aliens within our borders cannot be resolved quickly or easily. Faced with this situation, everyone—government officials and citizens alike—hopes to find a United States refugee policy which is both realistic and yet reflective of the humanitarian principles nurtured by the religious-ethical heritage of the nation.

Not surprisingly, some feel that recent events have overtaken United States policy and that the only thing we can do is to continue to muddle through as we have been doing; others are determined to search for a more consistent and coherent refugee policy in spite of the many difficulties involved. Certainly, government officials who are responsible for refugee affairs need all the help they can get in order to establish sound humanitarian grounds for sorting out claims of different groups who seek refugee or asylum status and to find the moral basis to give priority in group and individual cases. They must also consider whether the moral principles involved in dealing with the claims of asylees differ from those involved in dealing with the claims of established refugees. In the current political climate, and especially in view of the political relationship between the United States and certain nations, they must decide if it is realistic to expect the president or Congress to determine the relative weight of groups claims, or if there should be established something like a special court within the federal court system to determine status and to evaluate claims of particular individuals as well as groups.

Yet such policy issues, important and urgent as they are, touch only the initial phase of refugee problems. In order to deal with the long and painstaking process of the adjustment of refugees in their new environment and to insure a better relationship between refugees and local communities, government agencies on various levels, as well as private, religious, and welfare groups, must establish feasible procedures for cooperation and consultation. Moreover, the multidimensional implications of refugee/asylum issues demand that refugee policy be sensitive to other problems, from economic and educational to foreign relations, that affect the well-being of local communities and the nation.

# *Introduction*

## Alan K. Simpson

I am very pleased to be here. I commend the U.S. Coordinator for Refugee Affairs. I commend all of you, as you are the people who do the work. There is certainly no doubt that the refugee resettlement program in the United States originated with the churches and the voluntary agencies and that it would not get done without you. Our country's record on this is really one of our brightest achievements. We have, after all, brought into our communities over 600,000 Indochinese refugees alone, and most who have come in since World War II have assimilated successfully into American life and are loyal citizens and productive members of their community.

Nevertheless, the record number of admissions of the past few years, coupled with a resettlement program with a heavy emphasis on federal cash assistance, has generated some serious problems with regard to recent refugees, their sponsors, their host communities, and the federal agencies. You saw what we did this year. Instead of reauthorizing for three years, we reauthorized for one. The reason for this was so that we could examine some of the problems which are very apparent to such people as yourselves.

I have to deal in a legislative arena. You get the advantge of dealing in a more humane and compassionate arena. In the legislative sphere, we seem to deal always with short-term solutions. Thus we deal with the economic and political issues on the short term, while the longer-term social, moral, and ethical ideals sometimes go unattended. That is the way it is, and you have to know that, just as we know that yours is a different level of compassion. However, we hope that we have drawn up a generous, humanitarian refugee policy without being racist or mean. But it is not going to work unless it relates to the real world. If it did not do that, indeed, it would be irresponsible.

I have heard the term "backlash," and I have mumbled the phrase "compassion fatigue," not in a nasty way, but in a very real and honest way. The realities are that there are over 16 million people who have already pulled their feet away from their shores looking for a place to go. The U.S. cannot absorb them all; at least that seems to be the feeling in Congress. Yet we do accept more for permanent resettlement than any other country in the world. But we do have a problem. Look at the issue of the voluntary agencies and the high use of cash assistance. Look at the dependency rate, which varies from 51 to 91 percent in some areas of California. We have problems with taking a refugee to a sponsor or an anchor relative who is on public assistance and does not speak English and saying to them, "Thank you and here you are, God bless you. We will be back some unknown day to check on you."

The Congress is disturbed by that, and do you know why? Because our constituents say to us, "Wait a minute. You guys cut food stamps, and you cut welfare, and you cut job benefits for U.S. citizens, and yet you have a dependency network or a safety net for refugees which is greater and richer than anything." Take a look at what occurred the other day in the Senate with that amendment to remove Social Security benefits from illegal undocumented workers. I along with others moved to table that, but it was not tabled, by a vote of 34 to 58. That meant that a guy who was illegal but had two or three thousand dollars in the system was just written off. "So what," it is said, "he's illegal, what do we have to do with him?"

Let me tell you the toughest thing for me. The average American citizen and the average American congressman have no concept of the difference between a refugee, an immigrant, an asylee, a permanent resident alien, or a special entrant; he has no concept of any difference between those. His view of an immigrant is somebody that was kicked off the dock of Mariel Harbor and got to Florida and is dirty and tattooed and is picking up a weapon and trying to hack his way through New York City.

I have to live with that kind of concept, and there is a spirit down underneath that permeates and never surfaces, but it is out there. So I think we had best be about some kind of humane reform, because if we do nothing, I have some deep concerns about what could be the final result.

# Asylee and Refugee

## Michael J. Heilman

How is it that asylum has proven to be such a troubling issue? How is it that an asylum program, which is based on generosity and ethical considerations, has become the subject of acrimonious debate, seemingly endless legal proceedings, and congressional and executive disfavor?

It is tempting to respond that it is in the nature of asylum to produce discord. Certainly this has not been the case in the major countries of asylum and refugee resettlement. The aggravated nature of the debate in the U.S. is not a result of chance. It is a product of the asylum and refugee laws themselves, plus the values they are meant and thought to reflect.

The U.S. has the largest refugee resettlement program and the largest asylum demand in the world. Yet anyone listening recently would have the impression that we have the most restrictive and unfair system in the world. Given the programs which have been fashioned by statute and practice, it will not be easy to come to grips with the problem unless two events occur.

First, the structure and substance of asylum, as compared to the overseas refugee program, must be recognized. Secondly, there must be a concerted attempt by the persons who set the standards by which the program is judged to use terms and words which are more descriptive than polemical. An elevation of the level of discussion would tend to reduce the polarization which has come to exist and which has led, to a great extent, to the disrepute in which asylum is held.

The first step is to examine the asylum program in operation to determine its characteristics in the context of various political and practical pressures. It is in the elements of the program—some mandated by law, others the creation of expediency—that we find the flaws which cause the program to be so apparently irrational and unfair.

To start, it is best to outline the differences and similarities between asylum and refugee programs. It is important to know these characteristics because they are the framework to which we have attached so much emotional, ethical, and legal commitment. Of the *nine* salient features of asylum and refugee programs, there are two similarities and seven differences. The two similarities are in the refugee definition and the monetary benefits that flow from being granted asylum or refugee status. If a person seeking refugee status overseas, perhaps fleeing Vietnam, is able to make her way to a refugee camp, and is in the category of persons we have deemed worthy of interest, that person must, in theory, establish that she comes within one of the five types of persecution referred to in the Refugee Act refugee "definition." The same is true of a person who in the course of a stay in the U.S. finds himself stranded because a revolution or coup has occurred in his home country, as happened to thousands of Ethiopians a few years ago. Whether this definitional similarity means much in the end is an open question, because the definition in its bare form is one thing; the standard of proof applied is another.

Likewise, persons fortunate enough to be granted asylum or refugee status are entitled to the same social welfare programs. Again, this is a similarity without much substance, as refugees, particularly those from Southeast Asia, could not, by and large, come to the U.S. without such assistance. The typical asylum applicant does not need significant financial assistance and is employed by the time asylum is granted.

It is in the differences between asylum and refugee programs that we find the most significant elements. A person hoping to be granted a travel document as a U.S.–bound refugee must overcome major hurdles before she can even be considered. Most of these obstacles are entirely beyond the would-be refugee's control. The paramount factor in the overseas refugee program is the stark reality that the door is closed to most persons before they can even apply. The Refugee Act provides mechanisms to prevent large numbers of persons from swamping the system. It has long been a tenet of refugee policy that the

U.S. cannot absorb all, or even a good portion of, the entire refugee population in the world, often estimated at five million or more. In recognition of this truism, the Refugee Act allowed for curbs on admissions both structurally and quantitatively. There are no such limitations on asylum, a fact to which no small significance attaches, particularly in the light of the recent history of the Caribbean and Central America.

What are these brakes on the refugee process? Foremost is the limitation on numbers which may be admitted. This is accomplished through the statutory consultation process carried out in the autumn. More accurately, it is carried out prior to the formal congressional-presidential consultation, which merely formalizes what is usually a compromise number, arrived at through negotiation with the two judiciary committees. The consultation number sets the context for the next step.

The "next step" is also something of a formality, as it probably has been determined to a great extent what the refugee admission numbers will be. In any case, this step requires a determination as to which persons in the worldwide refugee pool are of "special humanitarian concern" to the U.S. This interest defines both the groups and the geographical regions from which we will admit refugees. If you are not of interest, you will not come, no matter how objectively compelling your case may be. For several years, Southeast Asia has produced the lion's share of refugee admissions; the question here has been how many will come, not whether we have an interest in Laotians, Cambodians, or Vietnamese. Other groups and regions are not the beneficiaries of this general consensus. As to Africa, the view has been that refugees will be resettled on that continent, because that is the best course of action for those refugee populations. Another example would be the case of Iranians outside of Iran after 1979. Although many had compelling claims, there was no interest in aiding them; more recently, refugee admissions have been begrudgingly allotted.

Assuming that a person is fortunate enough both to be of interest and to have an available number, the path to admission is still difficult. There is only one way to enter the refugee process. For most, this is through a refugee camp; for a few others, it is possible to apply at a limited number of consulates or embassies. The application process is fairly rigorous and can be quite time-consuming. For the vast majority of applicants, the process occurs within the context of a refugee camp, after a wait of months or years. After screening by various organizations and formal biographical interviews, an applicant will be presented to an immigration officer for a qualifying interview.

This is the point at which the application is granted or denied. An applicant who fails here has no recourse, in most instances. Some applicants whose claims are denied are fortunate to gain the sympathy and assistance of church or refugee relief organizations. In those rare instances, a rejected application may be reconsidered.

This contrasts sharply, of course, with the process by which a person may apply for asylum in the U.S. Applications may be made again and again, and presented to immigration officers or immigration judges. A denied application may be appealed to the Board of Immigration Appeals and to federal courts. The applicant may be represented by an attorney and present evidence and witnesses at a full evidentiary hearing.

One of the more interesting differences between the asylum and the refugee process is that relating to immigrant eligibility. An applicant for refugee status overseas must, with some exceptions, show that she is not excludable under any of the applicable grounds under the general immigration laws. In other words, the refugee who is of special concern is required to pass the same tests as an intending immigrant, although most of the grounds may be waived if it is in the national interest to do so.

An asylum applicant, by contrast, may have any status whatsoever in the U.S. and be granted asylum. The grounds of ineligibility do not apply. This means in practical terms that a high percentage of asylum applicants are deportable for some reason under the immigration laws, whether for illegal entry or for some other more sinister reasons.

Assuming that the refugee applicant is successful in making her claim, and is destitute, as most applicants are, then the applicant must be accorded a sponsor. This is not the case with persons granted asylum. While both may enjoy social welfare benefits, only the refugee is viewed as a potential ward of the government. While this at first glance seems perfectly plausbile, and perhaps even magnanimous, it assumes that an asylee is well-established and free to cope with American society. This is not always the case. It might be useful at some point to consider this aspect of the two programs.

Finally, the Refugee Act once more appears to treat refugees and asylum applicants evenhandedly when it comes to the discretion to grant or deny an application. In actuality, no asylum applicant who establishes persecution, no matter how unworthy she may seem to be, will ever be made to leave the U.S. This situation exists because paralleling the asylum process in the U.S. is a second process which requires refuge to be given if the applicant establishes any of the five types of persecution identical to those claimed by an applicant for asylum or refugee status. This means that a person may make his way to the U.S. by fair means or foul, may have lived freely in another country which gave him refuge, and still claim the right of "witholding of deportation"—the right to refuge, with no other qualifications attached. No such open-ended escape exists for the refugee applicant.

What we see at the end of this outline is a refugee process substantially different from the asylum process. If we were to characterize them in broad terms, the refugee process is more controlled and more restrictive. The asylum process, conversely, is virtually uncontrolled from beginning to end and presents a body of law and practice so amorphous as to have an almost unsurpassed capacity for manipulation.

As these differences do not exist in a vacuum, it is useful to examine their consequences in practical terms. We can assume that a person who perceives himself threatened will act realistically to free himself from peril. If the economy of a country is destroyed, or the police and military forces of a country have deteriorated to the point that existence is quite unpleasant, then the person will leave if he can.

For persons in the Caribbean or Central America, the country of choice for refuge is the U.S. Other countries may serve as temporary way stations, but the pattern of flight for most is to the south and southwestern U.S. If one is to be an exile, the most attractive place to go is a nation with a comparatively high standard of living. One would also presumably gravitate toward a society whose values are compatible. As a practical matter, it is also easier to go to a place where illegal presence is seldom detected and where family or friends can provide assistance. For good or for ill, the U.S. offers these advantages.

There is a certain irony in the fact that American society as a whole offers a good place to hide out, because the border crossers are greeted with something less than hospitality by the federal government. It takes no great mental prowess for a person to perceive this official hostility. If it was not known to him before he left his home country, it will quickly be communicated to him once he enters or at the border, as he waits to enter. We thus have a situation where persons look to a society for refuge but fear the government of that society.

When the characteristics of asylum join together in this context, certain reactions take place and certain perceptions, pressures, distortions, and temptations are created. This catalytic reaction is true for both the honest and the dishonest refuge-seeker. Remember that if the person has never been in a category of special interest to the U.S., then the refugee process has never been an option. If he has been, but numbers have been exhausted, then the person is also out of luck.

The result is that, in practical terms, for the vast majority of persons in refugee-producing situations who have access to the U.S. the refugee program is of no benefit. Asylum is always available. This leads to a situation in which persons are continuously fed into the asylum option category. As American society offers a place to disappear without difficulty and the government is hostile to persons who claim asylum, surreptitious entry is encouraged. This fact breeds further antagonism and also serves to discredit the asylum process in both the executive and legislative branches, since legitimate refugees form a portion of the larger migration of persons seeking entry simply to obtain employment.

The public response is ambivalent. It appears that a good portion of the news media reports on the problem faced by asylum applicants and border crossers from countries in turmoil, with a significant amount of sympathy. Church and aliens' rights groups quite vocally champion their cause, sometimes as a part of a larger campaign to discredit U.S. foreign policy, to which they are antagonistic. Because of this and because many of the border crossers appear to be victims of misfortune, there is a substantial reservoir of public sympathy for them.

In other instances hostility may arise, as in Florida with the Mariel Cubans and Haitian boat people. Along the southern border, to the extent that refugees are part of the overall pattern of migration, there is a perception that the borders are sieves. The refugee flow is simply viewed as one more piece of evidence that immigration is out of control.

The upshot of all of this is that asylum is in disrepute. This official view from the executive branch is that the asylum process is mightily abused. In part, this attitude is symptomatic of a larger disillusionment with the immigration laws and the manner in which they are administered. Congress is more divided on the issue, as is usually the case. There are some congressmen who would severely restrict the whole procedure because they consider the process overblown. Others are unhappy because they perceive unequal treatment of different groups for reasons which they consider totally improper, such as race or the desire to avoid offending a particular foreign government.

As events build one on the other, a chain of frustration is forged. The asylum process is an open process. Large numbers of people logically use it, for valid and invalid reasons. The more the process is used, the more it is officially resented, and the more suspect the motives of the applicants become. As more and more applicants are met by a cool or hostile reception, the tendency to avoid the process altogether becomes greater. This usually means that a number of asylum applicants appear only when they are in deportation proceedings and have exhausted other methods to remain. Because the readily approvable applications are granted prior to a deportation or exclusion hearing, the applications which end up being presented in this context are the most difficult, the most time-consuming, and the most likely to be hotly contested and publicized. This further feeds the point of view that the U.S. is being victimized by asylum applicants presenting bogus claims.

Differences of opinion over how to handle asylum claims have degenerated into rather poisonous debates conducted publicly and in the courtroom. The more the viewpoints have become polarized, the more the terms and words used by the various parties to the controversy have departed from a useful description of the situation, to code words used to express a particular social or political philosophy.

For example, a denied claim is equated on the government side with a "frivolous" claim, or a fraudulent claim, or further evidence of abuse of the process. At the other end of the spectrum, a denied claim is seen as evidence of political manipulation, or political oppression, or a flagrant violation of the law for partisan political purposes.

Likewise, some groups see all persons from any particular country as refugees. This has been the case most recently with Haitians and Salvadorans. The word "refugee" becomes a political statement in opposition to the ruling regimes in those countries. Used this way, the word gains a certain amount of respectability because it is close to the common usage of refugee, although bearing little resemblance to the specific term used in the Refugee Act. A refugee in common parlance is a victim of natural or manmade disaster, forced to leave home and country to seek shelter among strangers. Both Haiti and El Salvador appear to most Americans to be unattractive places of poverty or violence, or both. This is why the use of the word in this manner is not immediately perceived as inaccurate.

The obverse of this is the view that all persons from a particular country are "economic migrants." Haiti and El Salvador again offer useful examples of the use of terms as weapons rather than as descriptive and neutral devices. That this term is overly broad is readily apparent; it lumps a British interior designer in Manhattan with a poverty-stricken Haitian or a Cambodian peasant who has journeyed to Thailand in search of food. The term, in short, covers a host of circumstances.

To the extent that terms are used inaccurately and the speaker knows this, a question of ethics is clearly involved. The justification for the use of inaccurate or emotionally freighted language is probably plausible: the person views it as a useful tool in a worthy cause. The fact remains that it is still dishonest. It is also a self-perpetuating phenomenon, which tends to devolve into a more aggravated stage as time goes by, and the terms used escalate as stakes and emotions grow. I would like to suggest that it is time to break this cycle. A philosophy that the end justifies the means is peculiarly out of place as far as asylum is concerned, as the basis for an asylum program is basically a moral decision to aid the oppressed. To adopt a profoundly amoral philosophy to assist them is particularly offensive. The most offensive use of the asylum program occurs when applicants are viewed as vehicles to make political statements about the U.S. or another country, without regard to the merits of the claims presented. This practice can only serve to cheapen the asylum process. It is also obnoxious because it mixes true asylum claims of people who have suffered torture or imprisonment with cynical and dishonest claims which are made for the sake of expediency. People who use the process in this way are showing a vigorous contempt for the real sufferings of others, and are taking advantage of generosity in a calculating and fraudulent manner. Persons here today can influence the public discussion of asylum and refugee issues and can help establish standards of acceptable discourse. This is an ethical duty to the extent that the concept of asylum is a valued expression of moral values. Though we are far from abandoning our asylum and refugee programs, they have been subjected to severe strain by intemperate language. Asylum in particular is susceptible to damage because of its open-ended nature. Quite clearly, any process that allows any number of any persons, at any time, in any status, to apply, must rely for equilibrium on persons who make the applications to make the claim in honesty. Attorneys and church and aliens' rights organizations which represent aliens should all keep this fact in mind. Intemperate actions simply invite intemperate responses.

In this brief presentation, my purpose has been to outline the differences between asylum and refugee programs which tend to create pressures on the asylum process. These differences are, by and large, creations of statute, and it consequently is not possible in most cases to work around them. There is one exception, which I would simply like to pose as a possibility. To the extent that official disfavor results from the disorderly nature of the asylum process, it might be useful to make adjustments in the refugee process. This is most particularly the case with applicants from Central America and the Caribbean. Refugee programs could be established for people in these regions so that the asylum option is not the only possible route to the U.S. This would of course be a prodigious political undertaking, so I only wish to offer it as a suggestion.

Most of the differences between the asylum and refugee processes, however, will remain, in the absence of legislative revision of the Refugee Act. Because the asylum process required by law is so uncertain by itself—to say nothing of its fragility when contrasted with the refugee process—it requires a certain amount of discipline by persons who use it or counsel its use. At a minimum, it requires an honest use of its provisions and an understanding of the limits of the process.

# The Churches and Refugee Policy

## Charles C. West

Let me preface these comments with a quotation from Ambassador H. Eugene Douglas.

> Admittedly, here again, as it does so often, refugee policy raises a fundamental philosophical problem. Between those motivated by a redemptive compassion, who would grant asylum to all who manage to reach our shores and for whom there is a sponsor, and those motivated by no less noble principles, who would confine refugee policy within the limits of a foreign policy based on national interest, there is a tension that cannot be resolved once and for all. In fact, this tension is part of the fabric of American society and of the American political system. We have to live in a multipolar ethical environment at home just as we have to live in a multipolar political world abroad. (*Strategic Review*, Fall 1982, p. 17)

The ambassador is right in identifying in these words a fundamental tension in American society as it affects refugee policy. I would make only one amendment. The tension is not between people with different motives but within each of us. It is the tension between the believer in us and the citizen, between the command and promise of our faith and our responsibility for the national welfare, between the concern of the church and the concern of the state. I have been asked to speak here from the perspective of the Christian church and shall do so. Let me say to begin with, however, that this does not destroy the tension. The church is universal. Its center is not in the U.S.A. Its concern must be the world and its needs. But within this the welfare of the country of which one is a citizen has a relative, legitimate place. Redemptive compassion has a role to play in helping Americans to understand and redefine the national interest. If we lose hold of either pole of this tension, we fall short in our obedience to God and our responsibility to our neighbor.

Given this, let me suggest three angles on the refugee problem.

*First*, the most fundamental approach must be a ministry in the countries whose conditions produce refugees. The church, where it has been faithful, has always been clear about this. Christians are called to witness to the judging and saving power of God in every social situation and every country where they are. If there is political tyranny, it must be named and resisted for what it is, on the grounds where it holds sway. If there is poverty and oppression, the struggle for justice must take place there where the poor are. If tyranny and injustice have international roots, the people at home can count on the prayers and conscience of the church in other countries to support them in their struggle. But Christians, at least, are not called to flee from their responsibiltity to their neighbors, even inwardly in imagination, or to lose hope that God has a purpose for the country where they are.

For this reason, Christian churches everywhere tend to be bulwarks against mass flight from bad societies and at the same time tend to generate constructive action and liberating witness in those societies. This is true whether the oppression be of the left or of the right. Millions in the Soviet Union find humanity and strength for living in the Orthodox, Baptist, and Lutheran churches. In East Germany the Evangelical Church and in Poland the Roman Catholic Church lead their people in articulate, responsible critique of the policies of Marxist government out of concern for the true welfare of their nations. One could go on with many other examples. In Latin America resistance to right-wing dictators has its roots more often in the Christian church than in Marxist parties. The vision of the future may be socialist, due in no small degree to the perversity of American policy there, but the inspiration is Christian. In Southern Africa against white minority oppression, and in Ethiopia against Marxist rulers, a similar dynamic is at work.

In all of these and in many other situations, the church generates an indigenous witness and policy toward the nation's need. It does not generate refugees. Is this then a help to American national interest? In one way no, and in another yes. Where U.S. policy stimulates refugees, by encouraging flight from Eastern Europe, for example, through its propaganda or by backing governments, as in El Salvador, who make life intolerable for their people, the church and the U.S. government are of course opposed. But insofar as U.S. policy is concerned to promote human rights against dictators of left and right through its diplomacy and to practice a generous policy of development aid for poor countries seeking to build an economic base to support their own population (Haiti might be a test case in both respects), they may be allies.

*Second*, when all this has been said, we face the fact that refugee-producing situations explode from time to time because of factors over which neither the United States government nor the worldwide Christian church has much if any influence— Indochina, Afghanistan, Ethiopia, Uganda, Haiti, Guatemala, to name only a few. Mass escape from violence or chaos or from brutal repression is seldom a rationally considered choice or a moral decision. It happens in the force of circumstance, through the loss of home and community, the fear of death or of starvation. The refugees are all of a sudden there, in tens or hundreds of thousands. They pay very little attention to the social balance or the economic absorptive capacity of the countries to which they come. In their mass they seldom serve the short-term national interest of the country of first asylum. They may or may not have achieved any social virtue by struggling in their own country for justice and freedom. But they are human beings like the rest of us, and the first responsibility of the countries to which they flee toward them must be, in the words Ambassador Douglas used, "redemptive compassion."

Compassion, if we are to believe the Scriptures, belongs to the very heart and essence of what it means to be a people. "When a stranger sojourns with you in your land, you shall do him no wrong. The stranger who sojourns with you shall be to you as the native among you, and you shall love him as yourself, for you were strangers in the land of Egypt: I am the Lord your God"

(Leviticus 19:33-34). The theme runs like a binding thread through the law and the prophets of ancient Israel. It interweaves with concern for the poor and the oppressed as a sign of the integrity of Hebrew society, a matter not of generous charity but of right. "You shall not pervert the justice due to the sojourner or to the fatherless, or take a widow's garment in pledge, but you shall remember that you were a slave in Egypt and the Lord your God redeemed you from there" (Deuteronomy 24:17-18).

The New Testament too is full of such signs. Christ was born on a journey, a refugee in the first days of his life, executed outside the gates of the city, and as such has become the Lord and the Savior of every nation. Compassion for the refugee, if one reads this message aright, is like justice for the poor: the test of a nation's integrity. It is a testimony to the fact that all human existence has a temporary or sojourning quality, and that this fact hides a blessing from God for the national existence.

Let us be clear what this means. It is human need that has priority when the refugee floods pour over us, over and above consideration of the national interest, or concern about dislocations in our economy and way of life. Only by this compassion can Americans, paradoxically, preserve that reputation for openness and hope which is worth more to our national interest throughout the world than any number of military bases or business contracts. Our generous image, as Leo Cherne put it earlier, has a price. This is it. Furthermore it is present human danger that matters in determining who is a genuine refugee, not some subtle analysis of the motives for flight. The U.N. protocol adopted by the U.S. Refugee Act of 1980 is on the right track in defining a refugee as one who has a "well-founded fear of persecution on the basis of race, religion, membership in a particular social group, or political opinion," if he or she returns to the homeland. But the terms must be generously interpreted to cover all the cases. There are refugees from Guatemala and El Salvador who have had to flee simply because of where their home village is. There are Haitians and Cambodians who have become enemies in the eyes of their governments simply by the act of flight. It is present danger and human need, which set the terms of the refugee policy that is expected of us as a nation. By our response to these we will be judged. Compassion is in the deepest national interest.

But there is risk and sacrifice involved, and we have fears that make them bigger than life. We may be exploited by people who come here not for refuge so much as for gain. The job market may be flooded with low-earning foreigners. Our welfare systems may be overtaxed, our schools and public facilities overloaded. Our standard of living may fall. Our culture may be diluted by large doses of Hispanic influence. Even our policies may be changed by new ethnic pressures. These fears are based on real symptoms. Like all fears they can blow symptoms into trends and trends into dominant forces—unless there is something redemptive in the situation that can put the fears into perspective. But this is the point: there is.

Christians, I suppose, may be more inclined to believe and say this than others. Redemption has a special meaning in our theology. It means first what God has done and is doing through the death and resurrection of Jesus Christ for all who turn to him. We know how our own self-will, our greed, our anxious self-protection that sees our neighbor as a threat, are overcome by divine action. We hear about it in every church service. We partake of it in every Eucharist. We practice it in every prayer. It is not surprising that we should discern it at work in the world. God is a redeemer. This is the first reality with which we reckon and which we are called to trust, also in the politics of dealing with refugees.

But this is not just a religious perception; it is a secular fact. As such it ought to modify our politics. Let me illustrate.

Our fears tend to prevent us from seeing the refugees for what they are. They are, to cite Leo Cherne's figures, one small class of immigrants to this country, one-fifth of the number who enter legally by other channels each year, and perhaps one-tenth of the number of entrants whom the Immigration and Naturalization Service cannot verify as having departed. But they are a special class. They are not, on the whole, wandering opportunists seeking individual gain where they can find it. They have been torn from their homes by fear and danger, by forces beyond their control. They have left their possessions, their communities, their friends and often their loved ones—in short, a large part of their selves—behind in the homeland they have had to flee. They may well be torn in conscience too, for they have had to leave the burden of the struggle in their own country for others to bear. Theirs are devastated lives for whom the question is posed in stark human terms: How can they be redeemed? For what future can they hope?

The answer for them cannot lie either in simply forgetting the land from which they came, or in remaining an indigestible foreign body in the country that gives them asylum. They must learn to live creatively in the tension between two cultures, to adopt the new society that accepts them and become its loyal citizens, but never lose their hopeful responsibility for the society they left. We have seen this over and over again in our country. Refugees granted asylum tend to become the most patriotic of Americans; at the same time they feed into the lifeblood of America that deep involvement with foreign culture and society by which we grow and develop as a nation, in the world community of which we are a part. The result is that through them American society as a whole becomes more sensitive to the complex relations, the struggles, the hopes and fears—in short, the humanity—of other nations, including those we label as our enemies. This can happen through all immigrants, of course. It is the story of America's development from the beginning. But it is the special calling and contribution of the refugee just because of the violent, often involuntary nature of his displacement in the world.

Examples of this abound in recent history: the role of the German refugees in reconciliation with that country after World War II; the role of Polish, Hungarian, Czech, and even Russian refugees in sensitizing our country to the real situation in those lands today; the place of Chinese refugees in reestablishing our long-interrupted ties with their old homeland; the massive involvement with Latin America which each new refugee wave from there deepens—and one could go on. On the deepest level it is structures of peace that are here being built.

Then let us turn the picture around. It is not only the refugee that needs redemption. We as American citizens do, too. For our health on every level—spiritual, economic, political, cultural— we need to be challenged at the very center of our existence by the foreigner in our midst, not just by the ones we choose for their education and talents, but by the poor who are sent to us. The ancient Hebrews knew this well. Because the stranger in their midst was a sign of their covenant with God, they too could be a covenant witness to all the nations. "For out of Zion shall go forth the law, and the word of the Lord from Jerusalem. He shall judge between the nations, and shall decide for many peoples; and they shall beat their swords into plowshares. . . ." Anyone in this room could complete that quotation. We may never be worthy of that model. It was a hope and a dream for Israel as well. But in a secular and relative way we are being changed as a nation when we welcome the refugee. We are being taught how to be better neighbors, how to use our power in the world more wisely, how to feel the need of the poor more directly, how to relativize our fears and moderate our interests, in short, how to create bonds of peace.

*Finally*, what could this mean for immediate policy? Let me suggest a few measures. They are taken largely from church reports and from Christian and Jewish voluntary organizations. They are not comprehensive, but they do represent the policy direction we advocate. In some cases they are continuous with what the government is already doing; in others they propose an improvement on it.

1. The United States is cooperating with the United Nations High Commission for Refugees and with voluntary international organizations in a continuing resettlement program. This program should be developed and expanded, and the United States' part should be larger than it is now. At the moment so few refugees receive permission to settle in the United States through this program compared with those who find their way here first and seek asylum, that many who have had to flee their countries are encouraged to bypass it altogether. Yet the refugee problem is international. No one country should bear a disproportionate part of the burden.

2. Our government should expand and speed up the process of first asylum hearings, especially for refugees from Latin Ameica, and should pay more attention to current status and need than to the original motives of the refugee. At the moment there is an enormous backlog of applications, and great hardship

is created by long delays and by judgments which are more legalistic than humane.

3. It should be clear that refugees who are granted asylum should have full rights in American society, short of the right to vote which comes with citizenship. This should include the right to welfare in case of need, to education, to social security, and other entitlements. Furthermore, it should be recognized that refugees in this country before asylum decisions have needs in these areas which must be met.

4. Extended voluntary departure status has been granted to visitors from overseas legally in this country who would be endangered if they returned home at the expiration of their visas, but who do not wish to apply for asylum because it would cut off relationships with their home countries and therefore the chance of returning later. This category should be expanded and applied especially to Salvadorans and Guatemalans now in this country who would like to return home as soon as they can do so in peace and security.

5. Let us accept the Haitians who are in this country, regardless of how they came, while we work through every diplomatic and economic channel to change the conditions in Haiti which drive its citizens to risk their lives in open boats on the sea to escape from their homeland.

These are a few suggestions. There are doubtless many others. But there is one final word to be said. If churches expect the United States Government to be more open and generous in its refugee policy, they must themselves practice this openness and commend it to all the people in the country. Government finally cannot resettle refugees and integrate them into the common life. Only the people themselves can do this. The success of any refugee policy, then, depends upon the informed intercessory prayer with which the church makes present to itself the needs of displaced people around the world. It depends on the churches' willingness to educate the communities where they are in the challenge and opportunity of welcoming and helping refugees. It depends on structures of sponsorship, financial support, help with employment, and friendship circles which only voluntary groups, churches and synagogues among them, can provide. It is our job to provide the ethos as well as the advocacy which will make a generous American refugee policy work.

# Moral Considerations:
## The Value of Human Life*

## Marc H. Tanenbaum

My experience on three fact-finding missions with the International Rescue Committee to all of the refugee camps in Southeast Asia literally changed my life. My exposure to the Cambodian problem began in December, 1978, when I went to Aranyaprathet, which was among the first major camps in Thailand that received several thousand Cambodian refugees.

I walked through the medical clinic and saw some 125 men, women, and children in that desolate clinic starving—children who were bags of bones, with bloated stomachs, hair turned orange by virtue of protein malnutrition. I saw a mother who was a starved wraith of a person, and yet going through the ritual of putting the flap of her breast into the mouth of a child, although she did not have enough nourishment to sustain her own life. Both of them collapsed and died. And I saw one physician and one nurse running through that clinic trying to ward off death, in most cases unsuccessfully.

That was an experience whose only antecedent for me was Bergen-Belsen and Dachau. There were the same starved bodies, wracked with fever and disease, of Jewish men, women, and children. The only difference now was the pigmentation of their skin.

As an American Jew, as a Jew, I came away from the Nazi experience with an obsession that is an obsession for most Jewish people today; it is epitomized in a paraphrase of a verse in the Book of Leviticus: "You shall not stand idly by while the blood of your brothers and sisters cries out to you from the earth."

It is simply inconceivable that we are here calmly discussing statistics and conventional approaches as though this were just

-107-

another social problem. It is inconceivable to me that forty years after the Nazi Holocaust the international community can respond so blandly to the destruction of millions of human beings in Cambodia and elsewhere, and then consider casually—as if it were a daily weather report—the horrendous fact that if this food is not gotten through in the next few months, some 200,000 people will die, and by extrapolation an estimated two million more people may well perish before our eyes within the period of the next several years or so.

I simply cannot understand how the international community can go on with its conventional affairs and not feel the urgent sense that the sanity of mankind is at stake here.

That really is the issue—whether the human community can continue to indulge the conceit of regarding itself as sane and civilized and endure the reality that there are now several million people desperate for food and haven, whose very lives hang on having food brought to their mouths now, at this moment.

The world refugee problem is enormous. A total of 12.6 million people were refugees from their homelands or displaced from their homes wihthin their native countries ("internally displaced peoples") at the beginning of 1981. While in recent months the world's attention has been focused on the plight of Southeast Asians—the Vietnamese boat people, the Cambodians, the ethnic Chinese, among others—the most tragic, "life-threatening" refugee problems today are to be found among the 6.3 million refugees and displaced persons on the African continent.

According to the "1981 World Refugee Survey" published by the United States Committee for Refugees (on whose Board of Directors I am privileged to serve), the worldwide refugee total dropped 3.4 million over the last year, because of the improving situation in Southeast Asia, where millions of Cambodians who were displaced by war and famine have returned to their farms. But in Africa, whose fifty-three countries number among the poorest in the world, the number of refugees and displaced persons jumped from 4 million to 6.3 million as a result of political turmoil, religious-ethnic-tribal conflicts, and a spreading catastrophic drought. Africa today has one refugee to every seventy-five people.

About a fourth of all Africa's refugees are in one country—Somalia. More than 1.5 million people have crossed the borders of this small country (with an original population of 3.6 million) seeking refuge from the war between Somalia and Ethiopia over possession of the arid Ogaden region. The land they are leaving, as well as other East African countries—Ethiopia, Djibouti, and Sudan—is in the grip of a persistent drought which has forced thousands of people to move for survival.

In this barren region of northeast Africa there are now some 3.9 million refugees, and they represent one of the world's largest concentrations of suffering peoples. Except for the major international relief agencies and the Christian and Jewish refugee agencies who are involved in seeking to bring relief to these tragic human beings, the plight of the Somalian and other African refugees is virtually unknown to most people. Tens of thousands will surely die before the world wakes up and responds adequately in time to save their lives.

In Southeast Asia, there are still 700,000 Cambodian refugees in camps in Thailand and on the Thai-Cambodian border. In addition, the flight of Indochinese to other Asian countries persisted through 1980 and 1981. More than 160,000 refugees escaped from Vietnam and Laos, among them an estimated 75,000 boat people. The flow from both countries continued at a rate exceeding 10,000 a month during the early months of 1981. (Since 1975, more than 1.6 million refugees have survived their flight from Vietnam, Laos, and Cambodia. The number of those who died during the exodus is huge, probably in several hundreds of thousands, although there is no way to count them.)

It should be noted here that the response of Catholic, Protestant, Evangelical, and Jewish leaders and institutions to the Southeast Asia tragedy was one of the glorious chapters in the history of these religious bodies in this century. Since 1975, some 400,000 Southeast Asians have been resettled and rehabilitated in the United States alone, and seventy percent of these human beings were sponsored, resettled and rehabilitated—restored to their human dignity—by such groups as Lutheran Relief Service, Catholic Relief Services, Church World Service, World Vision, and the American Jewish Joint Distribution Committee and the Hebrew Immigrant Aid Society.

That lifesaving program was a translation into human realities of the basic biblical affirmations of the dignity of human life and love of neighbor that is inspiring in itself but, equally important, is a paradigm for our future collaboration in seeking to humanize the conditions under which so many millions of fellow human beings are forced to exist, frequently through no fault of their own.

It should appropriately be acknowledged that Denmark, Norway, and Sweden rank among the top contributors to the United Nations efforts to help refugees, when measured on a per capita basis. (The United States accepted more refugees—677,000— than any other country but ranked fifth on a per capita basis. The U.S. also contributed more money than any other nation in refugee aid, but on a per capita basis ranked twelfth in its financial contributions. Israel accepted one refugee for every thirty-seven residents, and Malaysia, Australia and Canada also accepted more refugees per capita than the United States.)

In looking to our common work in this area of vital moral and human concern, we need to ponder our responsibilities for saving lives, not only in Africa but in Pakistan as well. Next to the Somalian refugees, the plight of 1.4 million Afghani refugees who fled to Pakistan after the December 1979 Soviet intervention represents one of the great tragedies of our time. To complete the picture of human tragedy, we should know of the magnitude of the world refugee situation: Asia and Oceania, 2 million; Africa, 6.3 million; Middle East, 3.5 million; Latin America, 240,000; Europe, 350,000.

The world hunger and population problems are also part of the refugee complex of problems. Despite the recent heroic efforts to provide massive food supplies—in which Christian and Jewish institutions also played a leading role both morally and practically—some 800 million people in Asia, Africa, and Latin America continue to starve or suffer from severe malnutrition. It is estimated that several million people will die from hunger during the coming year in the developing countries.

The world's present economic condition, Robert Heilbroner writes, resembles an immense train, in which a few passengers, mainly in the advanced capitalist countries, ride in first-class coaches in conditions of comfort unimaginable to the enormously greater numbers crammed into cattle cars that make up the bulk of the train's carriages.

For Western civilization with its liberal, humanitarian ideals, and for peoples with our unambiguous Jewish and Christian ethical heritages, to temporize in the face of the greatest moral challenge in the last decades of the twentieth century is to risk the betrayal of everything morally meaningful that we profess to stand for. What is at stake in the way we respond during the coming months and years to this unparalleled world famine is our capacity to arrest the cycle of dehuminazation and callousness to suffering that is abroad in the world, ultimately affecting all peoples. We need to set into motion forces of caring and compassion that are the singular qualities without which an emergent interdependent—and peaceful—world cannot be sustained.

The Christian and Jewish communities, I believe, in concert with other cultural forces in our societies, can make a distinctive contribution, namely the definition and articulation of a new "Ethic of Scarcity" for peoples in our Western (and other) societies. The Western nations, in particular, have been blessed since their founding with what appeared to me almost limitless natural resources and materials. We seem to have been living on a set of unexamined assumptions that constitute an "Ethic of Abundance" which has rationalized and justified endless consumption, self-indulgence, and permissive hedonism. The waste at our business and social functions—conferences, conventions, weddings, confirmations, bar mitzvahs, even funeral wakes—have verged on the scandalous, especially when seen against the background of the needs of the world's starving masses. We have in fact entered a new experience of growing scarcity of resources and energy supplies as a long-term permanent condition, and our nations require a definition of values and human priorities that will result in greater self-discipline, restraint, and a genuine motivation to share out of a more limited supply of the earth's goods.

The cruel irony is that there is the capacity to provide that food now. The whole issue of whether human beings will be kept alive or will die depends on politics and ideology. That is, it depends on whether we can overcome the tendency to carry on with business as usual, averting our eyes from the critical problems at hand.

In my perspective of moral philosophy, states and ideology are created for the sake of serving human beings. Human beings are not created for the purpose of serving the state or politics or ideology. To the degree that the international political conflict represents an obstacle to saving lives, to that degree does that conflict represent a central moral and human issue which world leadership must resolve. The saving of human lives is the supreme issue, not the shoring up of one or another regime.

As Leo Cherne has made clear, as the Catholic Relief Services and others have made clear, the food can be made available today. The funds have been allocated. But if we allow this issue to continue to be another routine political problem, it will be months before that food will be gotten through. That means that tens of thousands, perhaps hundreds of thousands, of human beings will die before our eyes, and to me that is a moral obscenity. I cannot see how the human community can allow that to go on without recognizing the price we will pay in moral anarchy.

The whole question of the value of life is at stake, and the whole meaning of human existence is at stake.

How many Nazi holocausts, how many genocides can the world endure and regard itself as worthwhile to continue?

It seems to me that it is absolutely essential that in addition to the extraordinary contribution made by the American people and Congress—whose record has been, I think, one of the most glorious chapters in American history in terms of reflecting the generosity of American people and concern for this issue—an initiative must be taken now, not two months from now, *now*, to bring about an emergency conference through the United Nations of the major nations of the world, including the United States, the Soviet Union and Vietnam and Cambodia and China, before whom the issue of life and death survival is put.

There was a conference in April 1981 of the international community regarding Vietnamest boat people. It did make a difference.

I am persuaded that we can create the kind of forum on which the eyes and ears and concern of the world will be focused. Resistance must be overcome now, not three months from now, and attention drawn to those nations standing in the way. To that end, we have discussed today a proposal for a meeting with the U.N. Secretary General. This is the time of the winter solstice, which is the darkest period of the year. But is is also a period of light, and in this moral darkness we must find a way to bring some light to these people by calling a conference shortly—it is a little more important than even holiday vacations—to make it possible for us to save as many lives as we can day by day.

In my work I travel throughout the United States. The American Jewish Committee conducts interreligious programs with Catholics, Protestants, Evangelicals, Greek Orthodox, Black churches, Hispanics, and Muslims in almost every city in the United States. I have been traveling through virtually every city in this country since I have come back from Southeast Asia, helping organize Christians and Jews in programs of sponsoring refugees, of receiving refugees, organizing programs for rehabilitation, jobs, housing, medical care, social welfare, education, legal aid.

I have never seen such a mood among the American people of care and compassion and wanting to be present to relieve the suffering and hurt of so many millions of people.

The Catholics, Protestants, and Jews in this country have already brought to this country 75 percent of the nearly half million refugees who have come here since 1975. Christians and Jews have become a "community of conscience," and with the leadership of Congress and groups like the International Rescue Committee, I think we can really make a fundamental difference in saving human lives and restoring some sense of personal confidence and trust and meaning about being a human being in the kind of world in which we live today.

# Closing Remarks

## Charles C. West

Rabbi Tanenbaum picked up on a theme of this morning by raising the fundamental question: Who are we as Jews and Christians? And who are we as a nation as well? He defined these in relation to the stranger, in particular to the stranger in our midst referred to in the Seder feast, which is a reminder to the people of Israel that they were strangers and aliens in the land of Egypt and that God had brought them out and made them a nation. But the feast also reminds them that the stranger in their midst is a sign of God's care and that, indeed, God himself is a stranger whenever they think themselves as being too settled. Thus, the message from Rabbi Tanenbaum is that we must all remember that we are strangers who have been brought together by a grace which is not our own, and that the test of the validity and moral soundness of our existence as church, synagogue, and nation is our openness and our willingness to embrace the stranger who comes in from outside.

As to my own contribution, I began with the fact that there is an inevitable and healthy tension between the perspectives of a church and the perspectives of any state, of any political agency, and that we should articulate this in a creative way. Then I suggested two things. First, that the church, in every situation, begins by asking, "What is the promised purpose of God for that situation there?" Even though it be a situation of political pressure and of great economic poverty, the church has a ministry to the people there, and God has a purpose for the ministry of the people there.

In doing this, the church universal, the church ecumenical, becomes a church which in its whole being works against those forces which make those people refugees. It tries to find them their vocation in the countries where they are, and this may be pro or contrary to American policy, depending on how much we like the societies in which the church is carrying out that ministry. In some places it may be of very great help and in other places it may be that the church will have to say no to our American sense of what a political structure ought to be, and that there is a vocation here to be a Christian and a socialist, or to be a Christian and a guerilla.

As for the other panelists, Mr. Heilman contrasted for us the refugee and the asylum process from the point of view of the operation of the INS. He explained how the refugee process is limited by a strict quota and by a special format which involves only a fifteen-minute interview after which there is no appeal. The asylum process is quite different, as it has to do with people who have already come to this country. If I understand him correctly, he said that refugees overseas tend to regard the selection process—the legal selection process which goes on overseas—as far less hopeful than the process of getting into the country somehow and then applying for asylum.

Senator Simpson spoke of the restrictive spirit which is in the Congress and gave us some examples and warned us that we have our work cut out for us in influencing public opinion so that his colleagues would be pressured toward a more liberal refugee policy.

Finally, let me come back to the challenge of the discussion, to what Rabbi Tanenbaum and I had to say in terms of the question: What is the relation of the stranger within to the stranger without? Are we paying attention to the refugee at the cost of paying attention to the poor in our midst, to the minority cultures and communities in our own midst? Are we using it as a kind of escape? Indeed, do the refugees who come in displace or make things harder for the disadvantaged in our country as a whole? I think it is left with us as a question. We must not allow that to happen; it would be contrary to the spirit of our faith to allow it to happen. If it does happen, then how are we going to combat it and combine an active concern for domestic social welfare and interracial community with an active and creative refugee policy?

# *Reflections and Suggestions*

# The Problem of Refugees in a Strategic Perspective

## H. Eugene Douglas

It is safe to predict that in the year 2000 human pressures on national borders, group demands for refugee status and resettlement, and individual appeals for asylum will still rank as major issues of domestic and international politics.

Migrations may not, in fact, be greater now than in the past. Experts are only beginning to keep a rough record of human flows across national frontiers, and parts of the phenomenon still tend to be obscured: for example, we do not know the actual size of illegal immigration into the United States. We can be certain, however, that the coming years will witness a greater public awareness than ever before of the plight of people who leave, flee, or are driven from their countries of origin. Much more attention will be paid to the causes of migrations. This means that the subject is likely to become politicized—either systematically or in reaction to events.

### Emerging Strategic Outlines of the Problem

The subject of migrations and refugees is ripe for discussion, then, in a global strategic context. It is difficult to see how the many and complex issues involved can be reconciled in anything but a global context. Or to put it another way: it is difficult to see how in the year 2000 the sovereign right of nations to control their own borders will be viewed as a right that can be enforced unilaterally over time. The control of borders, like the control of economies, will become more and more a matter of consultation (if not confrontation) and negotiation between nations.

We are only at the beginning of thinking of these matters in a strategic context. Here at home the public debate over immigration and refugees has heated up of late, but the debate in Congress, while clearly reflecting new, restrictionist pressures, has been relatively restrained. Internationally, the Federal Republic of Germany has taken an initiative in the United Nations to establish a "working group on States' responsibility for mass exoduses," but the initiative has stalled in the Office of the U.N. Secretary General. "Strategic" thinking on this subject has been the province of a very few experts, working for the most part well out of the public limelight.

Yet, the signs of difficult decisions ahead are not hard to find. Whereas five years ago the backlog of asylum petitions before the Immigration and Naturalization Service and the State Department numbered in the few hundreds, it is now in excess of 100,000. Canada, West Germany, and France have experienced comparable increases. Overseas the numbers seeking refugee status and resettlement in the United States have reached such proportions than an elaborate priority system has been instituted to maintain control. Preference now is given to those with close political ties to the United States, including former employees of the U.S. government, to family reunification and, where possible, to those who were educated in the United States.

A primary cause of these expanded claims for asylum and refugee status is the fact that certain governments today deliberately discriminate against, or stigmatize, substantial numbers of their own citizens because of their political views or their "class" status. Nothing heightened the awareness of the American voter to the pressures of refugee claims more than Fidel Castro's decision in April of 1980 to "let out" some 125,000 of his countrymen through the port of Mariel. To be sure, in the early 1960s he had already "invited out" nearly a million others, virtually the whole Cuban middle class. Exiling "dissidents" has been a feature of Soviet policy ever since the Russian Revolution, one copied by virtually all the Marxist-Leninist governments of Eastern Europe at one time or another. Now the practice is spreading to other parts of the world.

The numbers involved in the exodus from Mariel were only about a quarter of the number of Indochinese refugees who have resettled in the United States since the fall of Saigon in 1975. Yet, the Marielitos woke America up to the fact that this kind of action by governments may become more frequent with the spread of Marxism-Leninism in the Caribbean and Central America. And if it does, there can be little doubt that the American people will demand a much more spirited defense, including perhaps preemptive or prophylactic actions, against the perpetrators of what may be depicted as a new kind of invasion across our borders.

At stake is America's historic identification with its own immigrant and refugee roots. Fundamental questions of public morality and political philosophy are involved. If we hold to a "universal right" of people to emigrate from their homelands, who has the duty to provide them a new homeland? And what should be the rights of those whom we do accept as refugees? If, as aliens, they are granted the rights of full citizens, does this risk diluting the rights of citizenship? (Would refugees prefer to keep an alien status in order not to be drafted, for example?) On the other hand, are we willing to tolerate a new under-class in our country—either formally, by expanding greatly the new category of "permanent resident alien," or informally, as happens when we tolerate a large population of illegal immigrants? And what of the division of responsibility between the federal government and states and localities when it comes to sharing the costs of refugee resettlement or migrant welfare?

It is not my purpose to explore these problems here. But merely to list them strongly suggests that we may not be able to live with the phenomenon of mass migrations in a narrow, national context. They have the potential for creating dangerous new tension in our society and many others. It is only in a global context that we can hope to manage the pressures of migration and refugee generation that lie ahead.


*Refugees and Foreign Policy*

Refugee policy has always been in fact a component of foreign policy. Some analysts like to compare refugee and immigration policy to tariff or trade policy: just as trade policy determines what products from abroad, and on what terms, enter our country and become part of our domestic economy, so refugee and immigration policy determines what people from abroad, and on what terms, enter our country and become part of our society.

But the analogy ignores the crucial distinction between *refugees* and *immigration*, between the victims of political oppression and the victims of, or escapees from, economic circumstances. Admittedly there is a mixture of political and economic motivations in most applications for asylum or refugee status: studies of the Marielitos indicate that many were drawn out of Cuba by the lure of bluejeans and other consumer goods sent into Cuba as presents by relatives and friends in Miami's Cuban community. Most refugees leave their homelands voluntarily rather than as the result of a specific, governmental act of expulsion. But maintaining the link between refugee status and political oppression is still crucial; if individual rights were respected everywhere in the world, there would probably be no officially designated refugees. Trade policy, perhaps, can be framed largely in economic terms, but refugee policy cannot be framed thus without simply defining the problem away and risking damage to the basic principles which underlie our political process.

Ever since the League of Nations decided in 1917 to give official assistance to refugees from the Soviet Revolution, the Western democracies have sought to internationalize the problem of refugee acceptance and resettlement. This remains our policy and that of France, Britain, Australia, Canada, West Germany, and a few other Western democracies. Through such devices as the Universal Declaration of Human Rights, passed by the United Nations in 1948, and the 1951 Convention on Refugees, the Western democracies have attempted to broaden the international acceptance of refugees, but the burden of accepting permanent resettlement of refugees has remained with those very few Western democracies willing and able to guarantee the protection of human rights. And now no democracy or group of democracies can afford to take everyone who seeks asylum or refugee status.

Meanwhile in the United Nations, the Universal Declaration, rooted as it originally was in the concepts of human rights embodied in Western political practice, has been amended with concepts of social and economic "rights," many of which owe more to Marx than to Jefferson for their inspiration. The Third World nations, which now dominate the debates in the U.N., seem to argue that until the disparities in the wealth of nations are so reduced that the pull of the rich nations on those seeking refuge from dire poverty is greatly reduced, there can be no meaningful international action in defense of individual human rights.

It is true that the largest numbers of refugees in the world today reside temporarily in Third World countries, particularly Pakistan, Somalia and Thailand. Fostering regional resettlement of refugees is a key feature of U.S. policy. But the prospects for a significant increase in the number of countries willing and able to accept permanent resettlement are not good. We are left, then, with a very great burden on U.S. domestic and foreign policy.

I want to examine what this burden means today in several strategic contexts: that of Africa (particularly the Horn of Africa), Afghanistan, Southeast Asia, the Caribbean and Central America, and Eastern Europe. How in each of these contexts does refugee policy either complement or complicate foreign policy, and how is the human rights dimension being coped with? The objective here is to frame the discussion of this sensitive subject in real terms, illustrating the complexities involved and the dangers of acting on only a single input or issue, while ignoring competing and conflicting considerations.

## African Migrations and Policies

In Africa more men, women and children are eligible for official refugee assistance from the members of the United Nations than on any other continent. It is also one place where international cooperation in these matters works reasonably well. This is so because those African governments accepting refugees— Sudan, Somalia, Nigeria, Gabon, Cameroon, Tanzania, Botswana, among others—grant them almost automatic access to land and to such social services as exist.

This attitude reflects the extreme sensitivity of most African governments to the fact that their national borders were established more or less arbitrarily by colonial powers, generally ignoring tribal and ethnic lines. Far better than trying to reorder borders by force, these African governments say, is an international system which accepts resettlement of refugees who are persecuted in their countries of origin for their tribal or ethnic roots.

It is only in the Horn of Africa, specifically in Somalia, where refugees pose a serious strategic problem for the United States today. It is a problem greatly complicated by the rise of a Marxist-Leninist government in Ethiopia—a government which relies on Cuban troops and Soviet and East German advisers for its security.

The problem might exist, it is true, even with a friendly government in Addis Ababa. The flag of Somalia has five stars on it—one each for the former colonies of Italy, France and Britain, one for Northeast Kenya and one for the Ogaden Province of Ethiopia. All these are areas with significant Somali populations, and the flag is the symbol of the Greater Somalia sought by Somali leaders for generations. This irredentism, naturally, does not go down well with the affected neighboring states.

The United States is interested in encouraging sufficient stability in Somalia to permit that country's government to participate in the protection of our common strategic interests in the Middle East. But the refugee population in Somalia is so large that it constitutes a devastating economic as well as political problem. (Nobody knows the exact numbers, but the ratio of refugees to settled population in Somalia is among the highest in the world.) The international Communist presence in Ethiopia makes it likely that this refugee population will not be assimilated either in Somalia or back into Ethiopia in any foreseeable time.

The situation demands, among other things, continued material support from the United States to the refugees in Somalia. It also demands care in treating claims for asylum among the small but vocal group of Ethiopians who found themselves in the United States when the revolution occurred in their country. The present policy is to grant "extended voluntary departure" status to those who left before June 1981: this status stays deportation procedures for the group as a whole, subject to annual review by the INS and the State Department. If "extended voluntary departure" sounds like a bit of casuistry, it is. It is nonetheless necessary to permit civilized treatment of a group whose interests must be reconciled with the interests of U.S. foreign policy. The government of Sudan, which also harbors a number of Ethiopian refugees, is receiving direct support from the United States—support which is badly needed and fully deserved.

## The Case of Afghanistan

The largest single group of refugees in the world today is the more than two and a half million Afghans driven from their country by the Soviet invasion. This is also probably the most effectively managed refugee program in the world, with the government of Pakistan, the United Nations High Commissioner for Refugees, many voluntary organizations from Europe and the United States, and the U.S. government cooperating in remarkable ways.

The government of Pakistan, of course, bears by far the heaviest burden. The great mass of these refugees (one camp has a population greater than the city of Albany, New York) is made up of nomads who used to cross the border at certain times of the year and now have taken up permanent positions on the Pakistani side. But this is not a unified group, politically or socially. And as the inflow spreads from the border areas of Pakistan into the Punjab, the economic and political problems faced by the government of Pakistan are bound to magnify.

Pakistan is a major strategic ally of the United States, and again refugee policy must be the complement of a broader foreign policy. Very few Afghan refugees are asking for resettlement in the United States, and fewer still are being accepted under the priorities laid down by the Immigration and Naturalization Service with guidance from the State Department. But it remains imperative that the United States continue to supply, directly and through the U.N. High Commission for Refugees, significant material support for refugee maintenance.

We must continue to do this until there is an Afghan solution in Afghanistan—which means until there is a withdrawal of Soviet troops. We must make sure that we are no less dedicated to this objective than is our ally, the government of Pakistan.

## Refugee Tides in Southeast Asia

Our deep, twenty-year involvement in Vietnam and Laos, ending in defeat with the fall of Saigon in 1975, provides the context in which more than a million refugees from these countries were generated. It should be a matter of some pride that we found homes for more than half of these men, women, and children in the United States. In defeat we did our duty: we faced up to our responsibility to those who took up arms in common cause with us and were compelled to leave their countries when that cause was lost.

The continuing flows of refugees in Southeast Asia remain a serious and complex problem. The human tide from Vietnam and Laos has dwindled, but Vietnam's invasion of Cambodia, following the catastrophe of the Pol Pot regime there, has produced new spates. While the rate of resettlement in the United States has fallen from a monthly average of 14,000 persons in 1980 to a current level of 5,000 to 6,000, we will continue to have to accept some refugees from this part of the world for several years ahead.

The most important refugee-related strategic problem in Southeast Asia today pertains to the security of Thailand. While there are no recognized rights of first asylum in Southeast Asia, and despite centuries of ethnic and cultural animosities with its neighbors, some 187,000 Indochinese refugees were in Thailand as of the summer of 1982. Granting even temporary asylum for these refugees in the face of a hostile Vietnamese army on its borders and in Cambodia is becoming increasingly difficult politically and economically for the Thai government.

In early 1981, when 165,000 refugees were in "holding centers" in Thailand managed by the U.N. High Commissioner for Refugees, the Thai government closed its border with Cambodia. That policy has always excluded the possibility of local resettlement of refugees in Thailand. Refugees from Laos (about 31,000 in early 1981) were placed in an "austere" camp in Nakhon Phanom. Escapees overland from Vietnam, who never have been granted even temporary refugee status by the Thais, have been kept in a camp on the Thai-Cambodian border which is below the standards of even the "austere" camps at Sikhieu and Nampho.

U.S. concern for Thai security makes it very important that we continue to give material support for the maintenance of refugees in Thailand and continue to work with others to help gradually thin out the holding centers by finding resettlement havens for Cambodian refugees where possible, including in the United States when the refugees can qualify under U.S. law.

Refugees from Laos pose a different kind of problem. The plight of the hill people who inhabit the mountainous areas of Laos and Vietnam, the Hmong tribe particularly, is tragic. These people were among the bravest and most steadfast of our allies. Now the Communist governments of Vietnam and Laos, employing a deadly chemical warfare agent developed in the Soviet Union and called "Yellow Rain," are bent on a course of extermination amounting to genocide. The Hmong and related tribes, preliterate people clinging to traditional tribal values, are not good candidates for Marxist-Leninist "reeducation."

Between 40,000 and 50,000 of these tribal people have been resettled in the United States, mostly in California, Oregon, Minnesota, and Rhode Island. Despite dedicated and considerate help from voluntary agencies, assimilation has been very difficult for the Hmong, whose leaders in any case are anxious to preserve their tribal identities and traditions against the day when they can return to their mountain homes. Resettlement of the refugees in Southeast Asia close to their homeland, therefore, is almost imperative. Hopefully the international community will in the future provide support to the government of Thailand which is appropriate to permit a more permanent refuge for these people in Thailand.

The plight of Cambodian refugees will continue until the Communist authorities in Hanoi withdraw their troops from Cambodia and permit a Cambodian "solution" to emerge. Continued international pressure to this end is essential, including pressure from Beijing. Refugees will also continue to try to leave Vietnam. The authorities in Hanoi, like most Marxist-Leninist governments, are obsessed with dissidents and "class enemies." Many are now confined as political prisoners in "reeducation" camps, from which some are sent as indentured servants to work in the Soviet Union and Eastern Europe.

It would be foolish to pretend that the United States has any great influence over the government in Hanoi when it comes to human rights. Having won a war, the Communists in Hanoi have a hold on their people much stronger than do their counterparts, say, in Eastern Europe. But it would be foolish as well to extend diplomatic recognition to Hanoi so long as its troops are in Cambodia and so many of its talented citizens are in "reeducation" camps. In this strategic context, refugee policy again must remain flexible if it is to serve as an effective component of foreign policy.

## The Swelling Problem in the Caribbean and Central America

One of Fidel Castro's "achievements" has been to make the United States, for the first time, a country of first asylum for refugees. That happened in the 1960s when Castro declared virtually the whole middle class of Cuba "class enemies," causing a million of his countrymen to leave, mostly to Florida.

It is remarkable in retrospect that this singularly important event did not exert more influence on U.S. foreign policy than it did. Perhaps in the decade 1965–1975 we were too preoccupied with Vietnam, Eastern Europe, and the Middle East to comprehend what was transpiring to the south of us. Perhaps we were lulled by the fact that the earlier Cuban refugees did so well in establishing themselves in Miami, becoming a great credit to their new community and their new country. In any event, the much smaller exodus from Mariel in 1980 caught the U.S. government by complete surprise.

The Refugee Act of 1980 was passed by Congress barely days before the Marielitos began to arrive. In the shock and confusion of the moment, the government decided to bypass the new act and asked Congress for special refugee relief legislation instead. The legislation covered not only the Cubans, but also Haitian applicants for asylum at the time (both were granted special "entrant" status). When it became clear that Castro had salted the Marielito exodus with a few thousand inmates of his prisons and mental hospitals, the implications of our inability to control these events began to dawn on many Americans who hitherto had not been concerned about refugee affairs.

Calling ordinary criminals and mental patients "class enemies" and dumping them onto a neighboring country is clearly something that even a tolerant people like Americans are not going to abide. But this is only the beginning of the legacy of Mariel that remains to plague us today.

A profile of the Marielitos shows that many were products of Cuba's baby boom of the 1960s—men and women, often with connections with the Cuban community in Miami, who were looking for a better economic prospect as much as for a freer political climate. They were less "class enemies" or the victims of oppression than those who had preceded them to Miami. Rather they appear to have been, fundamentally, escapees from Cuba's shrinking economy. Despite an annual subsidy of some $3 billion from the Soviet Union, Cuba's national wealth has not grown over the past fifteen years. That there should have been a significant baby boom right after the imposition of Marxism-Leninism in Cuba is something worth pondering: the sudden redistribution of even a shrinking volume of national wealth may induce a temporary sense of security, with serious long-term effects.

It can be said, then, that most of the Marielitos share much the same kinds of motivations that have brought many Haitians to Florida at great personal risk. In fact, Haiti is a much poorer society even than Cuba, and the human rights record of the past two Haitian governments is regarded by Freedom House in New York as even worse than Castro's.

Had the Congress and the Carter administration chosen to handle the Mariel exodus under the Refugee Act of 1980, our present dilemma over illegal immigration from Haiti would be somewhat less embarrassing. For while Haitians here illegally at the time were granted "special entry" along with the Marielitos, I do not believe that they were then, or are now, legally eligible for refugee status as a group. The Marielitos arrived as the result of a specific act of the Communist government in Cuba, one in which the U.S. government acquiesced. The same is not true of the illegal immigrants from Haiti. The distinction is important in foreign policy terms. If we were to depart from our policy of treating applicants for asylum on an individual, case-by-case basis to allow group asylum for illegal immigrants from Haiti, we would open our borders to a host of other illegal immigrant groups claiming that their governments are engaged in wholesale persecution.

Admittedly, here again, as it does so often, refugee policy raises a fundamental philosophical problem. Between those motivated by a redemptive compassion, who would grant asylum to all who manage to reach our shores and for whom there is a sponsor, and those motivated by no less noble principles, who would confine refugee policy within the limits of a foreign policy based on national interest, there is a tension that cannot be resolved once and for all. In fact, this tension is part of the fabric of American society and of the American political system. We have to live in a multipolar ethical environment at home just as we have to live in a multipolar political world abroad.

Pressures on our borders from the Caribbean and Central America—particularly Mexico—make it certain that in the foreseeable future, as never before in the past, the United States government is going to have to maintain a foreign policy, including preemptive and prophylactic measures, which has as one of its objectives the protection of our frontiers against excessive illegal immigration. The tensions within our society resulting from illegal immigration could grow to dangerous proportions. The key is a policy which acknowledges the need for more restricted entry while preserving the concept of refugee status and the right of asylum.

Before considering further some of the requirements of such a policy, it is well to take one final detour—to Europe, where it can be said that the modern refugee "movement" began.

## The Flow from Eastern Europe

The Jewish communities of Europe can claim credit for starting the modern movement for granting asylum to and providing resettlement for political refugees. ORT (Organization for Rehabilitation and Training) was formed by the international Jewish community in 1898 to assist Jewish refugees from Czarist Russia to learn the skills and attitudes necessary to adjust to a productive life in Western Europe and the United States. ORT provides today a significant part of the vocational training in Israel that has aided Jews from North Africa and the Middle East to adapt to life in Israel.

The League of Nations, which established a High Commissioner to assist refugees from the Russian Revolution, failed to do the same for the Jews persecuted in Hitler's Germany. Germany, a member of the League, prevented that. But a committee of League governments did create a High Commissioner for Refugees from Germany in 1933.

In the 1930s, the U.S. Congress on more than one occasion refused to provide for the granting of asylum in the United States over and above the then strict "national origin" immigration quotas. Even those quotas were not filled in the depression years, when isolationism still dominated foreign policy. It was not until after World War II that U.S. policy finally recognized the existence of refugees apart from immigrants subject to quota. And not until 1965 were the "national origin" quotas abandoned.

The old labels and attitudes toward refugees which evolved in the 1920s and 1930s are reflected still in U.S. refugee policy. Thus, Jews leaving the Soviet Union are granted refugee status almost automatically by the U.S. government, even though they can leave the Soviet Union only because they are granted visas to go to Israel. If on arrival in Vienna they choose to go to the United States rather than Israel—and nearly 90 per cent at one point so chose—they are accepted without being subject to the priorities established by the State Department for refugee applicants from almost everywhere else in the world.

Beginning with the uprising in Hungary in 1956 and followed by the Czech uprising in 1968 and the more recent troubles in Poland, a new kind of European refugee was created. These were not by and large minority groups persecuted for their religion or "national origin." Rather, these more recent cases have left their countries stigmatized as "class enemies" or otherwise branded as undesirables by Marxist-Leninist governments.

Here the old labels and old attitudes do not fit very well. We cannot automatically accept refugees from Eastern Europe who leave their countries because of their membership in a "social group" the way we have accepted Jewish refugees from the Soviet Union. We have to ask whether our refugee policy encourages dissidents to leave Communist countries to the extent that the prospects for liberalization from within are diminished. Would it help the Solidarity movement in Poland to encourage members to flee their country and seek refugee status?

Increasingly among the Eastern European refugees, as among the Cuban refugees, many are fleeing the economic failures of Marxism-Leninism as much as the political oppression that goes with that form of government. In individual cases it is often impossible to isolate one set of motivations, the pull of the prospect of greater economic opportunity, from another: the push of oppression.

This new kind of refugee greatly complicates the nexus between refugee policy and foreign policy. It is not enough any longer, as it was before and during World War II, to rest the case on an internationally recognized right of emigration—the right to leave one's country of origin. No country has an internationally recognized duty to provide a new homeland for refugees: that comes only out of a perceived sense of national security or interest and out of the cultural ethos of democratic societies, both of which are factors subject to change.

*Refugee Policy and Global Strategy*

This brief *tour d'horizon* makes it clear that refugee policy, as a component of foreign policy, raises many different problems in different geographical contexts. In Cambodia and Afghanistan the existence of large refugee populations reinforces the objective of finding an "Afghan" or "Cambodian" solution to naked aggression on the part of the Soviet Union in the first case, and its close ally Vietnam in the second. There is no possibility of permanent resettlement or asylum for more than a tiny fraction of these refugees in the United States or even elsewhere. The solution lies in voluntary repatriation, and that will not be possible until the Soviet Union and the Vietnamese are forced to withdraw their troops from Afghanistan and Cambodia respectively.

Elsewhere—in Africa, the Caribbean and Central America, and in Europe—the link between refugee policy and foreign policy is more complicated. In Africa, the Caribbean, and Central America the link involves that amorphous concept called "development."

Sadruddin Aga Khan, whose thirteen years as U.N. High Commissioner for Refugees mark him as one of the world's leading experts on the plight of refugee groups, stresses the connection between development assistance and refugee generation. He has recommended to the United Nations an expansion of refugee-related activities in the U.N., including better information-gathering and an early warning system in situations where mass exodus appears to threaten—all linked to an expanded role for official development aid, both to those countries losing large population groups and to those on the receiving end.

His prescriptions deserve, and are receiving, close attention from the U.S. government, particularly for their pertinence in Africa. It is hard to see how the tensions in the Horn of Africa, for one example, can be mitigated without a large direct investment in developing the dry lands of the region so they can better support the existing population, to say nothing of future population growth. The resources for such an investment will have to come from outside the region.

President Reagan proposed his Caribbean Basin Initiative in part for similar reasons. He wants to encourage governments in the region to follow policies that lead to job creation and to increased national wealth. This can be characterized as "preventive" action, designed to discourage somewhat the flow of illegal immigration to the United States.

Mexico is perhaps the acid test. Realistically there is no prospect that the United States will be able unilaterally to protect its long border from the population pressures in Mexico. Simply put: unless Americans can be persuaded that a job created in

Mexico is just as important to our national security and welfare as a job created in the United States, the prospects for good relations with Mexico are very dim indeed.

The trouble is that development, as Eugene Black used to say when he was president of the World Bank, is a fickle process: it destroys old habits and attitudes toward life and work even as it creates new wealth and new opportunity. It can lead anywhere. In this context it can generate new flows of people quite as readily as it can stem the flow of illegal immigration. It is very risky to rely on development assistance as a central tool of strategic policy. To put it another way: to reduce the problem of refugee generation to a plea for more "foreign aid" is to engage in a form of Russian roulette.

Haiti is a good example. Haiti is among the leading recipients of "foreign aid" in per capita terms. The result has been more, not less, pressure from individual Haitians to seek refuge in the United States. Castro's government receives an annual subsidy of $3 billion from the Soviet Union, but the result is greater pressure to leave Cuba, not less. And we have to face the fact that if Castro were to leave the scene tomorrow, those pressures would probably increase, at least for several years. It is most difficult to see how the Soviet subsidy could be replaced by a sufficient volume of job-creating investments quickly enough to stem the pressure for a new, large exodus from Cuba.

Nor should we fool ourselves into thinking that any significant volume of Cubans now in this country will return to Cuba if Castro should pass from the scene. Parents will not go back and leave their children here. Children, reared in and adapted to what is still by all odds the land of greatest opportunity, will not easily trade the American promise for the uncertainties that would await them in Cuba.

The word "development," in its most general and benign meaning, is a modern synonym for the Judaic-Christian notion of "progress." And insofar as this is true, it unmasks the fact that almost all discussions of "development assistance" are rooted in questions of moral philosophy. In U.N. debates "development" has taken on the trappings of an ideology—and one which usually gives more aid and comfort to the "scientific socialism" of Marxist-Leninists than to the historical experience of development in our own country and other Western democracies. Development assistance in the U.N. debates is measured most often by the size of resource flows between the governments of rich countries to the governments of poor countries that proponents say is "needed" to affect an international redistribution of wealth. But as the British economist P. T. Bauer and many others have long pointed out, such measurements completely ignore the cultural ethos and individual skills needed to create new wealth and jobs in any society.

Oddly, there is a connection here with the situation we face in Eastern Europe today. Detente lost part of its appeal in the United States when it came to be seen as a "foreign aid" program for the Soviet Union. The spectacle of real resource transfers from the governments of Western Europe to the Soviet Union and the Eastern European governments—transfers disguised in the form of credits far below the market cost of money and far below the cost that Western governments themselves must pay for money—lies at the heart of President Reagan's efforts to persuade America's allies not to subsidize the natural gas pipeline from Siberia and other "development projects" favored by the Soviets. The result, the president argues, is to create dangerous illusions of dependence in the West and to encourage the Soviets to strengthen their hold on Eastern Europe while building up ever greater armaments. A by-product of this process is to generate ever more refugees from Eastern Europe as the Soviet and Eastern European economies become more distorted and the Soviet hold on Eastern Europe tightens.

The missing link in strategy—one which appiles to much more than just refugee generation—is that between "development" and a common allegiance to political liberty. This is not ideology: we in the West offer no pseudoscientific development strategy to the world. Rather, it is merely the reflection of our historical experience—the experience of Western democracies that economic activity is stifled by political tyranny on the Marxist-Leninist model, and that political liberty is the environment in which economies (e.g., job creation) grow fastest.

The existence of a Coast Guard cutter off the coast of Haiti whose duty is to discourage illegal immigration into the United

States is not a picture with which many Americans are comfortable today. Indeed, it should be a warning to us all—not least to our allies in Western Europe. If we continue to subsidize and encourage governments who are the prime causes of refugee generation, Western European governments may be forced to take similar actions to defend their borders. No country, not even the United States, has a duty to provide a new homeland for all who manage to escape tyrannical governments; none, in fact, can do that. And the fact that from Vietnam and Cambodia, to Afghanistan and Ethiopia, to Cuba and Nicaragua, the tyrannies spawning refugees today all bear the Marxist-Leninist label should galvanize us into a better understanding of the need to stand together in the promotion of political liberty.

Living with the problems and complexities of mass migrations in the near future demands a foreign policy that promotes democratic development, including a respect for individual political rights. Such a policy must counter Soviet expansion—limit Soviet options—everywhere our real interests are threatened. It must work to wean away client states from Soviet domination and to unmask the ideologues of Marxism-Leninism before they gain power wherever that is threatened.

Such a policy will not permit us to have done with the problem of refugees, but it can make that problem more manageable. It can, that is, if we continue to balance our preventive measures with our tradition of hospitality to bona fide refugees and asylees. In international affairs, as sometimes in football, the best defense is a good offense, and maintaining our tradition as a haven for legitimate victims of political oppression is an essential part of that offense. At the same time, we must view ourselves as the friend of individual rights beyond our borders, and lead our allies to take this stand alongside us.

One feels no comfort because of that Coast Guard cutter off the Haitian coast. Rather, one feels alerted to how important it is now to reassert our belief that political liberty and democracy are necessities, not ideals—just as necessary for others as for us.

# Some Reflections on Immigration and Refugee Problems

## Joseph M. Kitagawa

*When a stranger sojourns with you in your land, you shall not do him wrong. The stranger who sojourns with you shall be to you as the native among you, and you shall love him as yourself; for you were strangers in the land of Egypt. . . .*
*Leviticus 19:33-34*

I would like to begin my reflections by suggesting three plausible pitfalls which this consultation should try to avoid. First, we should not be too general or theoretical. Often the temptation for church groups in dealing with social, economic, or political problems is to look for ready-made answers in the Scriptures or in papal encyclicals and present hasty resolutions with a naive assumption that making a pious pronouncement will automatically take care of practical difficulties that lie in the way of resolving practical problems.

Second, we should not be too practical in the sense of simply asking how the church, on the national, diocesan, or parish level, can alleviate today the plights of particular immigrant or refugee groups, be they undocumented Mexican aliens in the southwest, Cuban refugees in the southeast, or Asiatic groups on the West Coast. Admittedly, these are genuine and existential problems to which American churches must be sensitized. But I hope this consultation will not spend all its time discussing the immediate issues only.

Third, we should not be too provincial in the sense of regarding immigrants and refugees as uniquely or solely an American problem. Obviously, immigrants in this country are emigrants from other countries who came here for political, economic, or religious reasons. This simply reflects the fact that what is happening in this country is only a segment of a worldwide phenomenon of human dislocation involving more than 45 million refugees plus numerous repatriates, expatriates, and émigrés scattered over every continent. And, unless we understand the inner dynamics of the global pattern of human dislocation, we cannot begin to understand the nature of the immigrant and refugee problem in our own midst.

Among all the issues before us, I hope this consultation will pay special attention to two objectives. The first is to deal with immigrants and refugees as a set of long-range policy issues. The immigrant and refugee problem is like the visible portion of an iceberg floating above water, under which are the stubborn realities of social, political, economic, cultural, and racial factors that keep the problem alive. Thus we should try to sort out the tangled relations between the problem of human dislocation and such issues as international relations, international commerce, immigration policies, and patterns of racial prejudice and discrimination, and examine them critically and analytically in light of the basic principles which we affirm, such as human rights, civil rights, social, economic, and political justice, and the Christian attitude toward interhuman relations. In my presentation, I will make reference to the issue of racial discrimination as an example.

The second is to deal with immigrants and refugees as a religious problem. It is easy for us to agree that the church must do something for these troubled peoples, must try to alleviate their difficulties and minister to their spiritual needs. It is more difficult for us to accept the notion that the church, which has learned in the past from certain experiences of the Jews, such as the Exodus, the Babylonian captivity and diaspora, as well as from the experiences of the persecuted early Christians, must today learn once again the profound religious meaning of human existence in the midst of the chaotic state of human society by sharing the agonizing experiences of contemporary immigrants and refugees.

Let us first take a cursory look at a brief panorama of human migration and colonization in order to place the modern problem of immigrants and refugees into a proper historic perspective.

As far as we can ascertain, the early history of humankind was characterized by a series of migrations of peoples traveling overland or across the sea. For example, as early as 25,000 years ago ancestors of the native Americans (Indians) started migrating from the Eurasian continent, crossing the Bering Straits into North and South America. Also, various tribes were constantly moving in the immense steppes of middle Eurasia, the seacoast around the Mediterranean, and in northeast Asia. Around the mid-second millenium B.C., the Indo-Europeans—the ancestors of modern Europeans, Persians and Hindus—started migrating to Italy and western Europe on the one hand and to Persia and northern India on the other. The *Iliad*, the *Odyssey*, and the Old Testament give us a glimpse of the migrations of the ancient Greeks, Phoenicians, and Hebrews around the Aegean Sea as well as along the eastern Mediterranean shores. It was taken for granted in the ancient period that the migration of an ethnic group into certain areas implied the wholesale transplantation of the social, political, and religious structure of the invading group. In the course of time, several great regional kingdoms developed, each competing with rival powers for the acquistion of territories, material goods, and slaves.

It is significant to note that a new motivation, that is, "cultural colonization," was initiated by the Greeks, who attempted to unify all peoples in the *oikoumene* or the "inhabited quarter" of the world by extending Hellenistic civilization and the Greek language (*koine*). It was this vision which motivated Alexander, a one-time student of Aristotle, to establish a vast cultural, political, and economic network stretching from western Macedonia to India. Although Alexander's dream was doomed to failure, the Oriental-Hellenistic culture thus developed remained for centuries as the framework for cultural development in the Mediterranean world with Rome as its center. Meanwhile, in the Middle East, the once-tribal Hebrew religion developed an ethical universalism under the influence of Persian Zoroastrianism and the prophetic movement. In the course of time Christianity emerged from within the Jewish fold, but soon developed its own universal vision and penetrated the Mediterranean world. In the East, half a century after Alexander's departure from India, the Buddhist King Asoka (r. 274–232 B.C.) established a vast empire with a vision of unifying the peoples and nations of the world by means of the Buddhist teaching (*dharma*). Also in the third century B.C. the "First Emperor," Shih Huang Ti, unified China, which soon came under the influence of Confucian universalism. Thus by the beginning of the Christian era there were three great political-cultural spheres, each with its own universalistic vision, namely, China, which considered itself the Middle Kingdom of the world with its Confucian universalism; India, with its cosmic vision as embodied in Hinduism and Buddhism; and Rome, the heir to Hellenistic cosmopolitanism, which was later amplified by the Christian vision of the unity of humankind.

A fourth universalistic political-cultural sphere appeared in the seventh century A.D. with the emergence of Islam, which was accompanied by another series of human migrations. Islam quickly conquered the historic Christian centers in the Middle East and confined Christianity to Europe. Although Christian forces in Europe regained control of Sicily and Sardinia in the eleventh century, and the Iberian peninsula a little later, the Byzantine Christian forces in the East were overpowered by the Seljuq Turks, a nomadic group from the Turkestan steppes, who incidentally gave a ready excuse for European Christians to undertake a series of bloody Crusades from 1096–1291. Then came the Mongols, who not only conquered China and Russia but also extended their invasion into Poland and Hungary. Also, the Mamluks, originally a Turkish slave family, became rulers of Egypt, while the Ottomans, a tribe of the Ghuzz Turks, defeated Byzantine forces in 1453 and established a great empire. By that time Islamic influence had begun to penetrate eastward—into the Indian subcontinent and Indonesia and into the borders of China.

*Pre-Modern and Modern Patterns of Migration and Colonization*

The sixteenth century ushered in a new era—the era of European domination of the world. A new page of history was turned when the Mongol rule of Russia came to an end in 1480, followed by the expulsion of the Moors from Spain in 1492 and the discovery of the sea route to India in 1498 by Vasco da Gama. In contrast to Confucian China, Hindu India, and the Islamic Middle East, which were then showing signs of stagnation, the enormous vitality of European Christendom was apparent in the emergence of the modern nation states, economic nationalism, and a new social structure as well as the Renaissance, the Reformation and Counter Reformation, and colonial expansion into the non-Western world.

The European colonial expansion brought about three kinds of results. First, there was European migration into North America, Australia, New Zealand, and parts of Africa, which became an extension of Europe, culturally and religiously. Second, parts of Asia, Africa, and the Middle East were subjugated politically and economically by European powers, but were not heavily settled by Europeans: hence their cultural and religious traditions were not replaced by those of the Europeans. Third, there were areas such as Central and South America, the West Indies, and the Phillippines where the mixture of Europeans and natives produced hybrid peoples and cultures.

It is interesting to note that the pre-modern pattern of European colonialism, undertaken principally by Spain and Portugal, combined the most blatant form of economic exploitation with fanatic religious motivation. In contrast, the modern phase of colonialism combined economic exploitation with the motivation of extending a pseudoreligion of secularized salvation, namely, Western civilization. It should be noted that modern Europeans, rejecting the medieval notion of the political state as subservient to the church, accepted the political community as the framework for the fulfillment of human personality and civilized life. Thus, much as the ancient Hebrews considered themselves the chosen people proclaiming the true religion, modern Europeans came to regard themselves as the inventors and bearers of true civilization. They propagated Western civilization for the edification of the "backward races" in the non-Western world.

In the eighteenth century, however, Pietists rejected this secularized view of the human being as the creator of cultural values.

Thus the initial ethos of modern Christian foreign missions, inaugurated by the Continental Pietists and English Evangelicals, ran counter to the spirit of secular European civilization. Nevertheless, during the nineteenth century, Christian missions in the non-Western world cooperated unwittingly with European colonialism by propagating Christianity as one—albeit an important one—of the constituents of Western civilization. The combined forces of Western civilization, the Christian missionary enterprise, and colonial expansion brought about enormous social, political, economic, and cultural change in much of the non-Western world by the end of the nineteenth century.

One of the unfortunate consequences of modern Western colonialism was the development of a sense of racial superiority among Europeans. That is to say, the prosperity brought by colonial expansion led many Westerners to feel that their civilization, their religion, their technology, and their socio-economic and political systems were successful because they belonged to a superior "race." Inevitably, the sense of racial superiority resulted in the ugly practice of discrimination based on color and race, which spread like a contagious disease wherever the West was in political or economic control—in Africa, the Middle East, the Americas, and Australia. Thus, for example, Chinese were not allowed to enter the parks in the foreign concessions on Chinese soil. And, long before *apartheid* became the adopted policy in South Africa, "white Australia" excluded all "colored" immigrants—a policy that came to be liberalized only in the 1960s. In short, modern Europeans came to understand the human race in terms of two levels: the "superior" Caucasians and the "inferior" colored races.

*American Development: Its Ideals and Realities*

In the history of human migration, by far the most extraordinary development took place in the United States. Of the estimated 63,500,000 Europeans who emigrated during the period 1820–1931, nearly 60% of them immigrated to the United States, while the rest went to Canada, Australia, New Zealand, Argentina, and Brazil, etc. This fact alone makes the United

States a very special case. Equally significant is the constant tension between its ideal of "one people" and the stubborn realities of racial discrimination that have characterized the American experience.

From the beginning the colonists accepted English as the common language and English common law as the framework for their communal life. The various ethnic groups who settled in the new continent—Dutch, German, Scots-Irish, and others, many of whom were white European Protestants—were soon absorbed into the social, economic, and cultural life of the colonies which were Anglo-Saxon in temper and orientation. Still, it was remarkable that by 1776 the people in the thirteen original states developed a consciousness of being "one people." They must have shared an overwhelming sense of the drama of history in which free men, guided by the Almighty, had the task of establishing a novel form of society based on democratic principles as articulated in the Declaration of Independence.

However, the events of the hundred years following independence fostered a sectional spirit which threatened the nebulous ideal of "one people." In this situation, the Constitution, which was adopted as the supreme law of the land, carefully tried to maintain an intricate balance between liberty and authority. Also, the seemingly conservative tenor of the Constitution was complemented by the more liberal ethos of the Bill of Rights. Understandably, what guided the new nation was not a concrete model of society or of any set of arbitrary doctrines. Rather, new forms of society and new principles were hammered out of the historic experience of the people. For example, it was not from any abstract principle but from the actual experience of different religious groups living together that the principle of religious liberty came to be accepted as a cornerstone of the democratic society.

Fortunately or unfortunately, Americans' understanding of racial equality, or rather their inability to understand it, was conditioned by their pre-American European experience as well as their American experience. That is to say, the early settlers brought with them the common European sense of the superiority of the white races. Thus after independence a large number of European immigrants were welcomed and absorbed into American society even though they were not Anglo-Saxon. But the general attitude of white Americans toward nonwhite people, which was negative to start with, was further accentuated by their struggle against native Americans (Indians) and their memory of Black people as slaves. The gulf between the descendants of white Europeans and nonwhite groups thus resulted in institutional and social forms of bigotry. The American Union, which Lincoln called "a magnificent experiment in democracy," was nearly ruined by the civil conflict which centered around the question of Negro slavery. And, notwithstanding Lincoln's Gettysburg Address and the Emancipation Proclamation, many white Americans never quite believed that the proposition that all men are created equal was applicable in the fullest sense to people other than themselves.

Ironically, the constant tension between ideals and realities has made many white Americans schizophrenic about race issues. Many of them sincerely believe in the freedom and equality of individuals, and they reject the notion that there is special virtue in ancestry. They hold that all individuals of however diverse backgrounds, if given equal opportunity, can be assimilated into the new way of life to strengthen and enrich this "one nation, indivisible." The drive toward assimilation, however, has brought about some strange results. For example, as Robert Maynard Hutchins once pointed out, though American life rests on individual differences, it produces the most intense pressure toward uniformity.[1] Another side of the same paradox is that those who are not readily assimilable for reasons beyond their control tend to be excluded from full participation in national and social life. Such a double-edged pressure, which on the one hand drives men and women toward conformity and on the other hand discriminates against certain groups of people, developed in the course of time a complex pattern of prejudice which became, for all intents and purposes, the accepted principle of social control, exercising gentle tyranny over various segments of American society. This pattern may largely account for the problems of immigrants and refugees among the American people, characterized as they are by a

mixture of selfless humanitarian instincts and intolerable insen-
sitivities to the plight of newcomers, especially those who are
classified as minority groups.

*American Attitude toward Immigrants and Refugees:*
*Policies and Practice*

One of the most shocking anomalies in America has been its
attitude toward and treatment of first-generation immigrants.
America has always prided itself on welcoming new blood from
other lands, and some of the more fortunate or skilled people
have been warmly welcomed. But many of the less fortunate
immigrants have faced a number of serious hardships in this
country. Their experience of frustration usually begins at the
borders or the ports of entry. Frightened by the unfriendly
reception, many immigrants seek companionship and practical
assistance in their own national or racial groups, which often
congregate in certain sections, and this in turn makes them more
unacceptable and unassimilable to general American society.
Thus the vicious circle continues. The procedure of naturalization, simple though it is for the better educated, is not easy for
many older or less educated people. Besides, the process of
naturalization takes time. Once naturalized, immigrants are
supposed to be transformed by a strange alchemy into full-
fledged citizens, but in reality naturalized citizens are usually
barred from meaningful participation in social and political
activities. Many of them, however, endure the hardships with
the anticipation that the lot of their children will be better than
their own. More tragic is the plight of members of minority
groups who are expected to demonstrate their supreme loyalty to
the American way of life without enjoying some of the essential
privileges of being Americans.

It is worth noting that in the beginning it was assumed that
only "free white persons" would constitute American society.
Statutes did not permit the naturalization of nonwhite aliens.
Also, among "free white persons," Jews and Catholics were
subjected to discriminatory treatment. For example, while as
early as 1656 the Jews in New Amsterdam were allowed to
secure their own burial ground, they were not permitted to stand

guard like other burghers until they insisted upon equal rights and finally persuaded the authorities. When the British took over New Amsterdam, the charter of liberties and privileges was made applicable only to those "who professed faith in God by Jesus Christ." Fortunately, the Duke of York, to whom New York was granted, decided to permit "all persons of whatever religion soever" to exercise it, and the Jews were able to build a synagogue.[2] But it was one thing for them to win the right to exercise their religion, and quite another thing for them to be accepted socially. Considering the fact that in 1820 there were fewer than 15,000 Jews in a total population of nearly 10,000,000 Americans, it is surprising how persistently they were exposed to slander, threat, and social segregation. During their mass immigration following renewed persecution in Russia in the 1880s and 1890s, Jews became a favorite target of the hate groups which even today still try to stir the emotion of the Gentiles against them.

Roman Catholics too have had a difficult time in America since the colonial period. From Massachusetts to Virginia, Catholics, especially the clergy, were suspected of a popish plot and other alleged crimes such as spying for the French and inciting the Indians. Their situation did not improve with the Revolution. Catholics could then vote only in Pennsylvania, Delaware, and Maryland, although South Carolina and Georgia granted the right of suffrage to Catholics in 1790 and 1798 respectively, and eventually other states followed suit. Even then, Protestantism was the only *de facto* religion that was protected in many states. Nevertheless, the Catholic population in America grew steadily from 30,000 in 1790 to 100,000 in 1818. A large number of Catholics migrated to the United States from Ireland and Germany during the period 1820–1860, and from eastern and southern European nations during the period 1860–1960. In the course of time, American Catholics not only gained some political and social equality, but also developed an effective organizational structure to combat anti-Catholic sentiment that still lingers in certain segments of the country.

Little needs to be said about discrimination against Black Americans who are the "colored race" *par excellence* in America. No doubt white Americans inherited the European view that the Black people were inferior and that they were destined to serve as permanent laborers to enhance white economic prosperity. Soon, however, the Blacks became a political issue in the conflict between the Northern and Southern states, and even after the Civil War remained the central issue in the states' rights controversy. What lies behind the Black problem is a tacit acceptance, by many Americans, of color as the symbol of the unofficial caste system that has developed in America. To be sure, Blacks acquired the right of naturalization in 1870, but their citizenship was effectively nullified by the iron law of the color caste system.[3] Moreover, such a voluntary group as the Ku Klux Klan managed to segregate Black Americans in the South by means of force, intimidation, and fraud. And a nonintervention policy on the part of the executive, legislative, and judiciary branches of the government enabled some states to maintain their discriminatory policies toward Blacks for many decades. For example, in 1910 the State of Virginia changed its definition of a Negro "from a person with one-fourth Negro blood to one with one-sixteenth Negro blood," but again redefined a Negro in 1930 "as any person in whom there is ascertainable any quantum whatever of Negro blood."[4]

The fact that such a pattern of racial segregation has existed for so long in this land of freedom can be explained, at least in part, by the series of legal fictions that had been devised to justify it.

## Legal Fictions

The case of the native Americans (Indians) might be mentioned here although they are not immigrants but are the original inhabitants of the land. Although in principle the American government from the beginning had respected the property, rights, and liberty of Indians, the passing of the Indian Removal Acts of 1830 compelled tribes east of the Mississippi to move to territory west of the Mississippi, which soon became the bloody battleground of Indian wars. Curiously, the Supreme Court declared that "the Indian tribes were not foreign states but were alien nations" and as such the Indian was not an American citizen within the meaning of the Fourteenth Amendment.[5]

Only in 1924 did Congress pass an act which granted citizenship to all native-born Indians, and the Nationality Code of 1940 affirmed their right to citizenship. The strange fact remains, however (as Milton Konvitz points out), that Indians are not citizens by naturalization or by the Constitution, but by special statute.[6] While their welfare has improved somewhat since the passage of the Indian Reorganization Act of 1934, many more steps are needed before these original inhabitants of the land can take their rightful place with dignity and social equality in American society.

In comparison with the Blacks and the native Americans (Indians), the discrimination against Asiatics is less stringent and more localized. Records show that there were fewer than 100 Chinese in America before the middle of the nineteenth century. With the gold rush in California in 1849, however, the so-called "pig trade," which kidnapped and illegally transported Chinese laborers, brought to San Francisco alone 108,471 Chinese before 1863.[7] Yet California politicians soon used the Chinese as a political issue and succeeded in excluding Chinese immigrants in 1902. Once the discrimination against one Asiatic group was successfully enforced with a legal façade, it was easy for pressure groups to campaign against other Asiatics. Thus, while the "Gentlemen's Agreement" of 1907 virtually stopped Japanese immigration, pressure groups continued to agitate against the "menace" of the Japanese. Finally, the Supreme Court decided in 1922 that Japanese were ineligible for American citizenship, and in 1924 Congress passed the Quota Act which officially terminated Japanese immigration. In the meantime, the 1917 barred-zone provision prohibited all immigration from India, Siam, Arabia, Indochina, the Malay Peninsula, Afghanistan, New Guinea, Borneo, Java, Ceylon, Sumatra, the Celebes, and various other parts of Asia.

Such wholesale discrimination against Asiatics was based on strange legal fictions. For example, in 1922 the Supreme Court chose to interpret the 1870 naturalization law to mean that only members of the white "race" were eligible for citizenship, and declared Japanese ineligible on the ground that they belonged to a Mongolian "race."[8] In the same year, dealing with a case involving a high-caste Hindu, the Supreme Court declared that the person in question was ineligible because, though he might belong to the Caucasian "race," he was not a "white person." The court stated that "the words of the statute are to be interpreted in accordance with the understanding of the common man from whose vocabulary they were taken."[9] This type of legal fiction was extended to the extreme by Mr. Justice Cardozo who declared in 1934: "Men are not white if the strain of colored blood in them is a half or a quarter, or, not improbably, even less, the governing test always being that of common understanding."[10] Even more strange is the legal ground on which the Filipinos came to be excluded from naturalization. Although they owed allegiance to the United States as American "nationals," they were regarded neither as American citizens nor as "aliens," and, because the Filipinos were not "aliens," so it was declared, they were not eligible for naturalization.[11]

Thus, during the period from the turn of the century to the 1930s, Asiatics were excluded from citizenship because of race, or color, or because they were not "aliens." And as the Asiatics, confronted by legal, social, and economic barriers, were forced to form their own communities on the West Coast, they were accused of being secretive, too industrious, clannish, or unassimilable. With the outbreak of World War II, Attorney General Warren of California quickly succumbed to the pressures of racist groups who called for the removal of all American citizens of Japanese descent and their alien parents; he declared that the absence of sabotage in the early months of the war was a positive indication that Japanese Americans had plans for a program of concerted sabotage. The climax came early in 1942 when the Commanding General of the Western Defense Command ordered all persons of Japanese ancestry—most of whom were American citizens—to be removed from their homes on the West Coast and to relocate in ten centers of concentration without due process of law on grounds of military necessity. "The Japanese race is an enemy race," declared General DeWitt, "and, while many second and third generation Japanese . . . have become 'Americanized,' the racial strains are undiluted."

Standing in contrast to General DeWitt's statement is the statement of General Emmons of Hawaii, made on December 21, 1941:

Hawaii has always been an American outpost of friend-
liness and good will and now has calmly accepted its
responsibility as an American outpost of war. In accepting
these responsibilities, it is important that Hawaii prove that
her traditional confidence in her cosmopolitan population
has not been misplaced. I wish to emphasize the fact that if
the courage of the people of these islands is to be main-
tained and the morale of the entire population sustained,
we cannot afford to unnecessarily and indiscriminately
keep a number of loyal workers from useful
employment.[12]

The absense of an evacuation of the great majority of Japanese
aliens and their citizen children from Hawaii, an area located at
the heart of the Pacific war, shows that the mass relocation on the
West Coast was the result of regional pressure groups.

The mass evacuation of 110,000 persons of Japanese ancestry
was a tragic, and yet logical, result of the pattern of racial
prejudice and the legal fictions that had justified it. That such a
colossal injustice could take place in mid-twentieth-century
America indicates the tenacity of the racism that has infected the
social, political, economic, and legal systems of our nation.


## Refugees and Other Aliens

Closely related to the issue of immigrants in this country are the
issues of refugees and other aliens, registered or undocumented.
Here again, what we are facing in America must be placed in
historical and global perspective.

Throughout history there have been numerous cases of human
displacement caused by wars or political upheaval and change of
national boundaries and/or sovereignties, which compelled
some people to flee from their homelands in order to escape
persecution or danger. While some of them managed to return
home after short periods, others were settled and incorporated
into the societies of adopted nations. For example, ancient
Sparta allowed such people to become the *Neodampdeis* (new
citizens) with certain rights and obligations. Ancient societies
treated temporary visitors and refugees variously, the injunction

of Leviticus 19:33-34 being one of the most humane examples. Records of famous historic cases of refugees, for example, the Moors and Jews who were expelled from Spain by the Christians, the French Huguenots who fled France in the sixteenth century, and the English Loyalists who escaped to Canada at the time of the American Revolution, show that they were eventually able to establish themselves in new environments in spite of the great difficulties involved.

The picture is radically different in the twentieth century both in terms of the vastness of the refugee population and the degree of difficulty they experience.[13] World War I, which left numerous Europeans homeless and forced many of them to become temporary refugees, was followed by the Russian Revolution, which drove 1,500,000 anti-Bolsheviks into exile. In the 1920s, 500,000 Greeks and 200,000 Armenians fled Turkey. Fortunately, under the leadership of the Commissioner for Refugees appointed by the League of Nations, some of the World War I refugees were resettled in various European nations and in North America. Then in the 1930s, the rise of the Nazis and the Fascist regimes in Europe and the militarist regime in Japan that resulted in World War II created a vast number of refugees and exiles, including some fortunate Jews who had survived the bloodbath.

It is reported that UNRRA (The United Nations Relief and Rehabilitation Administration), which was supported by forty-four nations, managed to repatriate ten million World War II refugees to their homes. Also, IRO (The International Refugee Organization), operated by the UN from 1947 to 1952, helped another ten million exiles from behind the Iron Curtain to resettle elsewhere. In fact, over 395,000 refugees have been admitted to the United States alone since the passage of the Displaced Persons Act in 1948. Unfortunately, subsequent events have multiplied the number of uprooted refugees, for example, the partition of India and Pakistan (1947) which involved mass migrations to and fro, the creation of the state of Israel (1948) which caused the phenomenon of Palestinian refugees, the partition of Korea (1948), the Communist takeover of Mainland China (1949) which resulted in the mass exodus of Chiang Kai-shek's followers to Taiwan and the exile of Tibetans to India, the Hungarian Revolution (1956), and the more recent events of the Cuban Crisis and the Vietnamese War, to say nothing of the incessant turmoil in Africa, South America, the Middle East and Southeast Asia. Moreover, we must expect many more such events and an increase of displaced persons between now and the year 2000, and like it or not the United States will play an important role in this process.

Confronted by such an immense human and political problem, the United Nations has created two agencies: UNRWA (The United Nations Relief and Works Agency for Political Refugees in the Near East) and UNHCR (The Office of the United Nations High Commissioner for Refugees) in 1949 and 1950, respectively. Apart from the United Nations, there are many governmental and nongovernmental agencies in various countries, notably the Intergovernmental Committee for European Migration. The United States alone has more than forty agencies, including CARE, the U.S. Committee for Refugees, and other voluntary and church-related groups.

Both on the international and national level, all these agencies and groups suffer from lack of adequate funding and the apathy of governments and peoples regarding the never-ending and ever-increasing problems of refugees. Three obvious observations must be made in this connection. First, the spontaneous act of good will on the part of government, civic, or church groups in helping fellow human beings in distress, commendable though it is, is not sufficient. It must be followed up by systematic programs of rehabilitation of individuals and groups of refugees in terms of the legal, economic, social, and human issues involved. Second, the problem of the refugees requires the closest coordination and cooperation between governmental and nongovernmental agencies, especially church groups. Third, those who are concerned with refugee issues must relate themselves not only to our own government and to the United Nations, but also effectively advocate their cause to regional governmental groups which are destined to play significant roles in solving cross-national problems, such as the European Common Market, ASEAN (Association of Southeast Asian Nations), and the Organization of American States, in promoting the welfare of refugees and in opening up the immigration policies of various governments.

As far as the U.S. is concerned, regional cooperation is essential not only for our immigration and refugee problems but also for the related issue of undocumented aliens. According to Mr. Leonel J. Castillo, Commissioner of the Immigration and Naturalization Service, close to 400,000 legal immigrants come into the U.S. annually, while approximately 15 to 30% of legal immigrants emigrate from this country, so that the net immigration is considerably less than the gross figure of 300,000. This is not an astronomical figure considering the size of the nation. Concerning the refugees, there is no estimated annual figure because of the very nature of the refugee problems, which occur when the U.S. is involved in affairs of other nations, for example, Cuba, Korea, and Vietnam, or when the humanitarian instinct of Americans responds to the needs of oppressed peoples elsewhere, such as Soviet Jews. This, however, is not a unique American problem; all civilized nations have tried to accommodate refugees, and the U.S. must do its share.

Much more difficult than the problems of immigrants and refugees is the problem of undocumented or illegal aliens. According to Mr. Castillo, in late 1977 an estimated three to five million undocumented aliens lived in the United States; about 60% of these were Mexican nationals. Although the average length of stay is unknown, that of Mexican nationals is about six months.[14] There is no simple explanation of why there are so many undocumented aliens in the country, nor is there any easy resolution of the problem such as repatriating Mexicans en masse as was once tried in 1954 under "Operation Wetback." On this point, Mr. Ivan M. Timonin, Director of the Immigration Policy Development, Canada Employment and Immigration Commission, suggests, using Marshall McLuhan's imagery, that illegal immigration is something like "the attempted transmission of a message when the medium is turned off." He goes on to say that this phenomenon takes place because, even in a time of serious unemployment, there are certain types of jobs available for Mexican laborers in the U.S. just as there are always certain types of jobs available in Canada for Newfoundlanders. If it is true, as I suspect it is, that certain business and agricultural interests in the U.S. are counting on Mexican laborers, measures should be taken to legalize the entry of some of them on a temporary worker basis, so that they could return home legally, inasmuch as many of them are males whose families remain in Mexico. No doubt the long range resolution of this problem requires basic policy decisions regarding immigration and temporary work arrangements between the United States and its immediate neighboring nations, balancing domestic economic conditions and America's interests in and responsibilities toward the regional community.

In the meantime, serious efforts must be made immediately on national, state, municipal, and community levels to understand the tragic condition of the Chicano minority in this country, and to improve the communication and relationship between Chicano groups and other segments of American society.

## Some Reflections

Earlier I pointed out that human history has been a history of peoples on the move, and yet the problem of immigrants and refugees is a peculiarly twentieth-century problem. Today there are numerous refugees, repatriates, expatriates, and émigrés, to say nothing of constant movements of immigrants crossing national boundaries. Unfortunately, the sheer magnitude of the problem of human dislocation makes most of us as individuals feel helpless, so that many people simply shrug their shoulders not knowing how to get hold of such a colossal problem. Also, we are inundated every day by news of revolutions, counter-revolutions, and armed conflicts which result in more refugees and émigrés in every continent, to the extent that our senses have become immunized, and we no longer feel the problem of human dislocation in its existential dimensions. Yet we must realize that the problem of immigrants and refugees is a matter of great importance to us both as Americans and as Christians. Let me, therefore, offer some random reflections on this problem as a modest contribution to this consultation.

First is my reflection as a citizen of this republic. Whether it is right or wrong, I believe that the utopian vision, which originally brought this nation into existence and which provided a rationale for the so-called "Americanization" movement after the outbreak of World War I, has lost much of its impetus in our time. The aim of that movement was to transform peoples of different backgrounds into "typical Americans," but in their eagerness the advocates of "Americanization" paid little attention to the complexity of the psychological, social, and cultural factors involved in the assimilation process. Moreover, some of the leaders of the movement were inclined to believe that only those of European backgrounds were capable of becoming "typical Americans." Ironically, therefore, a person could be both an enthusiastic integrationist and also a *de facto* segrationist simultaneously. This accounts for the fact that the problem of immigrants and refugees, which is closely related to the problem of ethnic minorities, cannot be understood without taking into account the existence of racial prejudice and discrimination in our society.

Understandably, the decline of the "Americanization" movement encouraged the view that the uniqueness of American democracy lay in its ethnic, religious, and cultural pluralism. Thus, no neat theory can easily explain the contradictory character of American society, which vacillates between the demand for uniformity and the reality of a *de facto*, uneasy coexistence of diverse ethnic, cultural, and religious groups. Caught by the ambiguity of this situation, both dominant and minority groups tend to resort to oversimplified stereotypes in their relationship to each other. What frustrates minority groups is the fact that the views of the dominant group alone have been considered "public opinion" for a long time. The stereotyped "public opinion" of the dominant group has kept alive discriminatory measures against certain ethnic groups and has influenced national policies regarding immigrants, refugees, and undocumented aliens. In a real sense, the pluralistic and even separatist mood of certain ethnic minority groups in recent decades may be seen as a reaction against the persistent pattern of discrimination, precipitated to be sure by the growing appreciation of their own ethnicity and cultural roots as well as by their aspiration for human and civil rights. Many of them ask today as Martin Luther King once asked: "What good is it to be allowed to eat in a restaurant if you can't afford a hamburger?"[15]

More recently some minority group leaders have begun advocating political collective bargaining rather than protest movements; some of them go so far as to demand not only civil rights but also compensatory and preferential treatment. When one translates such a demand into concrete terms such as special quotas or preference, it amounts to the proposition, in the words of Daniel Bell, "that rights and opportunities should inhere to one on the basis of [racial] group, not of individual, status."[16] This indeed is a complex problem for which there is no easy resolution. Dr. Charles Lowery, chairman of the admissions committee at the University of California–Davis which turned down Allan Bakke, admits that his committee had a difficult task deciding between minority and nonminority candidates. In his own words:

> I feel a lot of compassion for someone like Bakke, who is obviously qualified to go to medical school. . . . But, at the same time, I believe strongly in programs to recruit minority physicians. How are we going to make amends to our minorities for the long and bitter bias against them unless we start somewhere?[17]

Dr. Lowrey's statement reveals the dilemma that disturbs the consciences of many people who are concerned with social justice in American society, involved as it is with the rights, privileges, and duties of the members of the dominant group as well as those of the minority groups. Related to this is the question of how to protect the civil and human rights of recent immigrants, refugees, and undocumented aliens without inflicting undue hardship on the rest of the people in this country.

Second, as a Christian I take seriously the religious meaning of the problem of the immigrants and refugees. I am firmly convinced that whatever we do for immigrants and refugees, we must avoid the connotation of sentimental charity or covert proselytizing. From lobbying on their behalf for more humane and just national policies to providing them with immediate practical assistance, we must be motivated by the sense of justice at the bottom of Christian love that acknowledges the dignity of every person as a person, and from which follow every person's rights and obligations in the many dimensions of human relations.

More importantly, we should recognize that the global phenomenon of human dislocation in our time is not simply a political phenomenon; it is also a manifestation of the human spirit. Various peoples are determined to escape oppression and poverty because God has been at work among them all along in ways past our comprehension to bring about "release to the captives and recovery of sight to the blind, and to set at liberty those who are oppressed." Thus our religious and humane concern should not be limited only to those immigrants and refugees living within our borders but also should be extended to men and women in various lands who are struggling for their survival, liberty, and justice. As Charles Malik aptly stated:

> It is impossible for Christians not to pray for and bless every genuine attempt at dignity and independence, every craving for freedom and equality, every desire on the part of the peoples of Asia and Africa [and elsewhere] . . . to realize their potentialities to the full. These are as much the children of God, "created in his own image," as anybody else and Christ died as much for them as for you and me.[18]

Finally, I hope we as Christians have the capacity to see in the experience of the immigrants and refugees the paradigmatic meaning of human existence. Ironically to many of us spoiled as we are by the prosperity and comfort of our society, the troubles, sorrows, and mental anguish which characterize the experience of dislocated persons seem to be quite foreign. Moreover, our religious habit has been such that when we think of the church we cling to the memory of the grandeur of the Constantine model of the church—one of power, prestige, and influence. Yet the forebears of our faith community were those whose experiences were not unlike those of contemporary immigrants and refugees. Think of the imagery of walking (*halak*) in the scriptures—the wandering of Abraham, Isaac, Jacob, and their descendants walking from Egypt to Sinai, Sinai to the promised land, then to Babylon, and back to Zion! It was through their experience of being on the move, in the midst of their suffering, frustration, and dislocation, that they learned the sacred meaning of life and history. "Behold, I beseech you as aliens and exiles, . . ." says the first letter of Peter. This greeting was addressed not only to the small group of poor and persecuted Christians of the early church, but also to us in the twentieth century who have lost the sense of being pilgrims.

It may well be that the existence of the unfortunate victims of human dislocation—the immigrants and the refugees—is a reminder of the deeper meaning of human existence which we do not otherwise understand. Significantly the Gospel of Luke portrays the prototype of the church in the walking of two disciples on the road to Emmaus, "talking with each other about all these things that had happened." They felt so strongly about what they had heard and seen that they shared their experience with a stranger on the road who turned out to be Christ himself. We too are pilgrims on the road, and when we share our experiences with our walking companions, especially those who are immigrants or refugees, our hearts too may burn within us for the joy of discovering Christ on the faces of our fellow human beings who are tragic victims of our inhospitable society.

I have depended heavily on material from "Refugees," *Encyclopedia Britannica*, 1971 edition, in writing this paper. Also helpful has been Milton R. Konvitz's *The Alien and the Asiatic in American Law.*

*Notes*

1. Robert Maynard Hutchins, *No Friendly Voice* (Chicago, 1936), p. 1.
2. Sigmund Livingston, *Must Man Hate?* (Cleveland, 1944), pp. 134-135.
3. See Buell G. Gallagher, "Racism and Color Caste," in Clarence Tucker Craig, ed., *The Challenge of Our Culture* (New York, 1946), pp. 74-104.
4. "Negro, American," *Encyclopedia Britannica,* 1965 edition, 16:192.
5. Milton R. Konvitz, *The Alien and the Asiatic in American Law* (Ithaca, 1946), pp. 110-111.
6. Ibid., p. 113.

7. K. M. Panikkar, *Asia and Western Dominance* (London, 1959), p. 280.

8. Konvitz, p. 81.

9. Ibid., p. 89.

10. Ibid., p. 95.

11. Ibid., p. 93.

12. Cited in Bradford Smith, *Americans from Japan* (New York, 1948), p. 180.

13. The following figures are taken from "Refugees," *Encyclopedia Britannica*, 1971 edition, 19:71-72. I have depended heavily on this material in writing this section of my paper.

14. Quoted from *World Issues* (published by the Center for the Study of Democratic Institutions) 3, no. 2 (April/May 1978):16.

15. Quoted in William Julius Wilson, *The Declining Significance of Race* (Chicago, 1978), p. 13.

16. Daniel Bell, "Plea for a 'New Phase in Negro Leadership,'" *New York Times Magazine*, May 31, 1964, p. 29.

17. Dennis Breo, "Why Allan Bakke was turned down," reprinted from *American Medical News* in *Chicago Sun-Times*, September 24, 1978.

18. Quoted in *Advance*, November 1, 1954.

# Some Policy Suggestions Regarding Asylum

## Anthony J. Bevilacqua

I am grateful for this opportunity to share with you the very deep concerns of the Catholic Church in the United States in matters relating to mass movements of people to seek asylum in this country. Our tradition as a haven for the unwanted and oppressed has been heralded throughout the history of this nation. Events of the recent past, however, have presented new challenges which threaten the maintenance of that tradition. In this presentation we will make a number of positive suggestions directed at providing solutions to these new problems and hopefully ones leading to a restoration of our image as a nation and people imbued with humanitarian concern for all mankind.

In any mass asylum scheme the total population will be divided into basically two groups, those who will be crossing our land or sea borders in large numbers and those already in the country having been admitted with temporary visas. Our initial remarks will relate to the former group, for whom a comprehensive emergency preparedness plan must be developed. May we suggest that such a plan include the following:

1. The designation of a specific agency to manage and coordinate the delivery of all services to the population. Permanent funding authorization must be incorporated into the enabling legislation to facilitate an immediate response to the emergency.

2. A plan for the initial reception, temporary care including shelter, and transportation to permanent relocation sites.

3. The designation of permanent processing centers in various parts of the United States. Such centers must be readily accessible by good transportation to relatives, legal counsel, and voluntary agencies. Areas subject to extreme weather and temperature conditions should be avoided.

4. Health care and social services, including (a) adequate facilities for medical examinations and treatment on the site as required; (b) establishing nutritional food programs related to the population's traditional diet; (c) unrestricted access to the centers for religious functionaries who wish to administer to the spiritual needs of the people; (d) appropriate indoor as well as outdoor recreational activities; (e) the immediate establishment of English language classes and vocational training programs.

5. The guarantee of the right to representation by attorneys or representatives of recognized voluntary agencies. Since these services are customarily provided on a pro bono basis, every effort should be made to expedite the processing of all applications filed, thus saving time and money both for the government and counsel.

6. An asylum hearing process that is simple and expeditiously handled yet guarantees due processing of all applications. We endorse the concept of an asylum hearing officer, one who will be a specialist in the technique of interrogation (we hope bilingual), well-versed in judicial procedures and applicable law and possessing an in-depth knowledge of the economic and political conditions of the country from which the aliens have fled. We envision certain geographical or political area specialists who will receive on-going orientation and training relating to changing world situations.

While recognizing and endorsing the need for streamlining the asylum hearing process, we must insist on the right to an administrative appeal from an adverse decision of the asylum officer. Such an appeal should be directed to an existing appelate body such as the Board of Immigration Appeals of the Justice Department or to a newly created Asylum Review Panel. The latter might be composed of representatives of the State and Justice Departments, the Office of the United Nations High Commissioner for Refugees, voluntary agencies, and lawyers associations.

7. Early release from detention of all who do not pose a clear threat to the security or welfare of the country, with the assurance of expeditious processing. The treatment of all should reflect the humanitarian concern traditionally manifested by the United States for those seeking refuge here. That concern must

also relate to the length of detention, a matter presently the subject of numerous judicial proceedings in our courts, an inappropriate setting to our minds, for the determination of levels of compassion, hospitality or charity.

The conditions of release should not, however, relate to the posting of bonds. Release on one's own recognizance or parole to relatives, friends, or voluntary agencies should be utilized.

8. Resettlement assistance, including financial assistance to voluntary resettlement agencies and financial, medical, and social services to the aliens where needed. Such assistance must be made available not only to those granted asylum but also to others who for one reason or another cannot be immediately removed from the United States and whose long-term detention is unnecessary or unwarranted for financial or humanitarian reasons. The Refugee Act of 1980 is deficient in this respect even for those persons granted asylum status. The needs of asylees, especially those who have arrived in a mass movement directly from their country, are just as pressing as those processed abroad for entry as refugees.

We feel compelled to question the wisdom of undertaking a program of interdiction of vessels suspected of transporting undocumented aliens to our shores. The possible violation of international law and protocol will not be addressed here. The potential, however, for violation of individual human rights and danger to human life is clearly evident and of the most serious concern to us. We draw no parallel between the interdiction of vessels carrying suspected contraband cargo and those transporting human beings. Are we to equate material goods with human life?

We must express also our fears of the adverse effect this U.S. interdiction policy will have on those fleeing oppression in Southeast Asia. Has the memory of those refugees being turned away only to suffer death by drowning and starvation been dimmed by the passage of time? Should this practice be resumed by the countries of first asylum, we fear that the United States will not be as persuasive as in the past in convincing those nations the practice should cease. Are we to abandon our role as the leader of the free world and defender of individual freedom?

There is need also to develop a policy and then a mechanism for assisting aliens stranded in the United States as a result of upheaval in their country of origin. Visitors, students, businessmen, and other nonimmigrants often find it impossible to make a decision regarding a return, due to the uncertainty of the political or military situation at home. At the same time it is also impossible to maintain their lawful temporary status in the United States, due to many factors including the cutoff of funding from abroad. Faced with this dilemma, many violate the terms of their entry by taking up unauthorized employment to sustain themselves or are forced to file applications for political asylum merely to gain time to await a stabilization of events in their home country. A clear policy should be enunciated.

We would like to call to your attention the September 17, 1981, statement of the Administrative Board of the United States Catholic Conference on the status of El Salvadoran nationals temporarily residing in this country. It reads as follows:

> We are deeply distressed that the conflict among opposing factions in El Salvador continues at a high level. As a result, thousands of persons have fled that troubled country and others have been stranded abroad fearing for their very lives should they return at this time.
>
> In the United States these individuals daily face the threat of deportation by our government to El Salvador. Many are forced to apply for political asylum as the only means of seeking at least a temporary haven and unfortunately the vast majority of these applications are being denied.
>
> It is our feeling that while their country remains in such a state of turmoil, the citizens of El Salvador who are stranded in the U.S. should not be forced to leave when their very physical well-being, regardless of political philosophy, is in danger. We, therefore, urge that a moratorium be placed on all deportations to El Salvador, at least until such a time as the government in power is in a position to guarantee the safety of its citizens.
>
> It is our recommendation that in times of national calamity, military or political upheaval abroad, the nationals of the

affected countries stranded in the U.S. be granted temporary refuge until it is safe and possible for them to return home. In the interim, they should be granted permission, if requested, to take up employment so that they can sustain themselves in a lawful manner. Such a policy should react to a de facto situation abroad and should be implemented with the least possible delay.

While we seek the immediate adoption and implementation of these proposals, let us also urge that there be an awareness of the basic problems which are the causes of masses of peoples fleeing their countries of origin and residence.

I will conclude by quoting from a recent statement of my Committee:

> There is . . . need for continued and accelerated efforts on the international scene, aimed at providing political and economic climates favorable to the prosperity and rights of individuals. The ultimate goal should be to insure opportunities for human beings to share in the bounty of the world wherever they live.

This was a statement made by Bishop Bevilacqua, as Chairman of the ad hoc Committee on Migration and Tourism, National Conference of Catholic Bishops, to the House Subcommittee on Immigration, Refugees, and International Law, on October 28, 1981.

# A List of Contributors

**The Most Reverend Anthony J. Bevilacqua,** now Bishop of Pittsburgh, was Auxiliary Bishop and Director of the Catholic Migration and Refugee Office, the Diocese of Brooklyn, until recently. He also serves as Chairman of the Committee on Migration and Tourism, National Conference of Catholic Bishops. His articles have appeared in the *Jesuit*, the *Catholic Lawyer, Migration Study*, and the Center for Migration Studies series entitled *In Defense of the Alien*.

**The Honorable George Bush** is Vice-President of the United States. From 1971 to 1973 he served as U.S. Ambassador to the United Nations. He was Chief of the U.S. Liaison Office, People's Republic of China, from 1974 to 1975 and director of the U.S. Central Intelligence Agency from 1976 to 1977. He became Vice-President in 1981.

**Mr. Leo Cherne** is the Executive Director of the Research Institute of America and the Chairman of the Board of the International Rescue Committee, the latter an organization that assists those who flee from totalitarian governments. He is also the Vice-Chairman of the President's Foreign Intelligence Advisory Board. The many honors he has received include the Legion of Honor of France, the Commander's Cross of the Order of Merit of the Federal Republic of Germany, and the Freedom Medal of the United States.

**Mr. Roger Connor,** the Executive Director of the Federation for American Immigration Reform (FAIR), was trained at the University of Michigan Law School and is a specialist in environmental law. His articles have appeared in the *Wall Street Journal*, the *New York Times*, and the *Washington Post*, as well as other national newspapers. He has appeared on many television programs. Mr. Connor is well known as an advocate of immigration reform.

**The Honorable H. Eugene Douglas** is currently U.S. Ambassador-at-large and Coordinator for Refugee Affairs. From 1981 to 1982 he served as a senior member of the Policy Planning Staff for the United States Secretary of State.

**Dr. Richard Harrow Feen, Jr.,** special consultant to the office of the United States Coordinator for Refugee Affairs, assisted Ambassador Douglas and the Religious Advisory Committee in setting up the March conference and edited its proceedings, which will be published through the Government Printing Office. He has contributed articles to the *Miami Herald* and the *Washington Post*, as well as to scholarly journals. Entries in the volume marked with asterisks (*) are taken from the proceedings edited by him.

**The Reverend Peter Gomes** is university chaplain and the Plummer Professor of Christian Morals at Harvard University. He is an ordained Baptist minister and the preacher at University Memorial Chapel.

**Mr. Michael J. Heilman,** Associate General Counsel, Immigration and Naturalization Service, Department of Justice, earlier served as a staff attorney with the Board of Immigration Appeals in Washington, D.C. Mr. Heilman was a Foreign Service Officer for the Department of State and at one time worked at the refugee processing center in Athens, Greece.

**Dr. Joseph M. Kitagawa,** Professor of the History of Religions, the Divinity School, the University of Chicago, and also in the Department of Far Eastern Languages and Civilizations, the University of Chicago, is also past Dean of the Divinity School. During World War II he was in internment and relocation camps in New Mexico and Idaho. He received the award of Distinguished Citizen of Foreign Birth from the Immigrant Protective League. His many publications deal primarily with the history of religions and with Eastern religions. He served as rapporteur of the March conference.

**Dr. Martin E. Marty** is the Fairfax M. Cone Distinguished Service Professor of the History of Modern Christianity at the University of Chicago. He is Associate Editor of the *Christian Century*, editor of the newsletter *Context*, and coeditor of *Church History*. He is also a board member of the National Humanities Center, consultant to an ongoing project called "Health/Medicine and the Faith Traditions," and an editor of the forthcoming *Encyclopedia of Religion*, a Free Press Publication.

**Dr. Peter I. Rose,** Visiting Professor at Harvard University (1983-1984) is Sophia Smith Professor of Sociology and Anthropology at Smith College and a member of the University of Massachusetts Graduate Faculty. He is a specialist on racial and cultural relations. His numerous publications include *They and We, The Subject Is Race, The Ghetto and Beyond, Americans from Africa, Nation of Nations, Through Different Eyes, Strangers in Their Midst, Mainstream and Margins,* and the forthcoming volume, *Tempest-Tost.*

**The Honorable R. Richard Rubottom,** Commissioner of the Good Neighbor Commission of the state of Texas, earlier served as Assistant Secretary of State for Inter-American Affairs, 1956-60, and as Ambassador to Argentina, 1960-1961. His multidimensional career has included the Administrative Vice-Presidency of Southern Methodist University and the Presidency of the University of the Americas in Pueblo, Mexico. He is also serving as a member of the Texas State Bar Association's Immigration Committee.

**Dr. John R. Silber** is President of Boston University. He began teaching philosophy at Yale University, then went on to the University of Texas at Austin, where he chaired the Department of Philosophy from 1962 to 1967 and served as University Professor of Arts and Letters and Dean of the College of Arts and Sciences from 1967 to 1970. In 1971 he moved to Boston University, where, in addition to his presidential duties, he is University Professor of Philosophy and Law.

From 1960 to 1967 Dr. Silber served as chairman of the Texas Society to Abolish Capital Punishment. He was Vice-President of the Austin Commission on Human Relations from 1966 to 1967 and served on the board of directors for the National Humanities Faculty from 1968 to 1972. He has been active in numerous other educational and civic projects.

**The Honorable Alan K. Simpson** took his seat in the United States Senate in 1979, representing the state of Wyoming. He is chairman of the Veterans' Affairs Committee, a member of the Judiciary Committee, chairman of the Immigration and Refugee Policy Subcommittee, member of the Environmental and Public Works Committee, chairman of the Nuclear Regulation Subcommittee, and member of the Reform and Courts, Environmental Pollution, Toxic Substance, and Environmental Oversight Subcommittees. He coauthored the Immigration Reform and Control Act of 1983, the most comprehensive immigration bill presented to Congress in the last thirty years.

**Rabbi Marc Tanenbaum** is Director of International Relations for the American Jewish Committee. He has served on numerous presidential and United Nations commissions dealing with many issues, among them foreign aid, aging, and energy. He was an observer at the Second Vatican Council in Rome. Rabbi Tanenbaum has worked extensively on refugee relief efforts and human rights throughout the world.

**Dr. Michael S. Teitelbaum** is Program Officer at the Alfred P. Sloan Foundation. At the time of the conference he was Senior Associate of the Carnegie Endowment for International Peace. Previously he served on the faculties of Oxford and Princeton, as Staff Director of the Select Committee on Population for the United States House of Representatives, and as Program Officer at the Ford Foundation. He is the author of "Right vs. Right: Immigration and Refugee Policy in the United States," in *Foreign Affairs* (Fall 1980), and *Fear of Population Decline* (Academic Press, forthcoming).

**The Reverend Silvano M. Tomasi,** C.S., Director of the Committee on Migration and Tourism, National Conference of Catholic Bishops, is the President of the Center for Migration Studies in New York, as well as the editor of the Center's journal, the *International Migration Review*. He served as Vice-President of the Research Committee on Migration for the International Sociological Association. Among his many publications is *The Disposable Worker: Historical and Comparative Perspectives on Clandestine Migration*.

**Dr. Charles C. West,** Academic Dean and Professor of Christian Ethics at Princeton Theological Seminary, has previously served as a Presbyterian missionary in China; a staff member of the Gossner Industrial Mission at Mainz-Kastel, Germany; the Associate Director of the Ecumenical Institute, Bossey, Switzerland; and a Lecturer at the University of Geneva. He is past President of the American Society of Christian Ethics and the author of *Communism and the Theologians; Outside the Camp; Ethics, Violence and Revolution*; and *The Power to be Human: Toward a Secular Theology*.

**The Honorable Elie Wiesel,** Andrew W. Mellon Professor in the Humanities, Boston University, and a renowned lecturer, author, and philosopher, serves among other things as Chairman of the United States Holocaust Memorial Council.